SUSAN B. ANTHONY

Born: February 15, 1820
Died: March 13, 1906

From the time Susan B. Anthony was a young girl, she always believed, as did her Quaker parents, that women were entitled to the same rights and privileges as men. Never happier than when she was working as hard as she could, Ms. Anthony traveled all over the country, organizing meetings and lecturing on the rights—particularly the right to vote—of women. With Amelia Bloomer and Elizabeth Cady Stanton, this dynamic, tireless woman contributed all she had to secure the vote for women. A contemporary of abolitionists William Lloyd Garrison, Wendell Phillips and Frederick Douglass, Susan B. Anthony also marched in the forefront of the antislavery contingent. A crusader for human rights, Susan B. Anthony's story is one of great interest for today's woman.

BOOKS BY IRIS NOBLE

Biographies

CAMERAS AND COURAGE
Margaret Bourke-White

CLARENCE DARROW
Defense Attorney

THE DOCTOR WHO DARED
William Osler

EMMELINE AND HER DAUGHTERS
The Pankhurst Suffragettes

EMPRESS OF ALL RUSSIA
Catherine the Great

FIRST WOMAN AMBULANCE SURGEON
Emily Barringer

THE HONOR OF BALBOA

ISRAEL'S GOLDA MEIR
Pioneer to Prime Minister

JOSEPH PULITZER
Front Page Pioneer

MASTER SURGEON
John Hunter

NURSE AROUND THE WORLD
Alice Fitzgerald

SUSAN B. ANTHONY

WILLIAM SHAKESPEARE

Novels

COURAGE IN HER HANDS
MEGAN

Susan B. Anthony

By Iris Noble

JULIAN MESSNER
NEW YORK

Published by Julian Messner, a Division of Simon & Schuster, Inc.
1 West 39 Street, New York, N. Y. 10018. All rights reserved.

J
920
A

Library of Congress Cataloging in Publication Data

Noble, Iris.
    Susan B. Anthony.

    Bibliography: p. 179
    Includes index.
    SUMMARY: A biography of one of America's most outspoken
crusaders for human rights, particularly those of women.
    1. Anthony, Susan Brownell, 1820-1906—Juvenile
literature.   [1. Anthony, Susan Brownell, 1820-1906.
2. Women's rights]   I. Title.
JK1899.A6N6   324'.3'0924 [B]   [92]   74-30230
ISBN 0-671-32714-3
ISBN 0-671-32715-1 lib. bdg.

Printed in the United States of America

SUSAN B. ANTHONY

Chapter One

The chimes woke Susan to a guilty start. Five o'clock! Almost before the last sound died away she was out of bed and across the dark room. Dawn had not yet lightened the square of windowpane. She had to light the candle before she could see where she was going and what she was doing.

In front of the washing stand she poured ice cold water from the pitcher into the basin, and scoured herself with a coarse cloth and towel before getting into her petticoat and dress. She yawned. Six o'clock was her usual rising hour, now that she was twelve years old, but this was no ordinary morning, and her mother needed her help as quickly as possible.

This was the glorious day in the late summer of 1832, when the Anthonys would be moving into their new, beautiful brick house. Her father would supervise the final touches, but the women folk had to get the food ready for all the friends and neighbors and hired workmen who would be assisting Daniel Anthony.

Already Susan could hear busy movements in the kitchen below. Milk pans rattled. The plunger thumped against the wooden bottom of the butter churn. Brisk footsteps moved from table to fireplace to pantry. The mouth-watering smell of freshly-baked bread came up through chinks in the bedroom floor.

Washed and dressed, Susan tiptoed over to the bed where her sister Hannah still lay deep in slumber. "Get up, Hannah," she said, shaking her. "Thee will be late. Let Mary sleep; she is only five years old and it is too early. I will call Daniel."

There was no need to call him. Her eight-year-old brother met her on the stairs. His hair was wet, his eyes bright, his face scrubbed. "After today," he gloated to Susan, "I'll have a room to myself." It had been hard for Daniel to share his room with six of the brickmakers, who kept him awake with their snoring.

Oil lamps burned in the kitchen, adding light to the roaring fire in the fireplace. In one corner of the room Grandmother Read rocked baby Eliza's cradle with the toe of her slipper, while her elderly hands were busy spinning thread on the wheel. Sister Guelma, two years older than Susan, was churning butter. The center of all activity was Mrs. Anthony, who put a kettle on the fireplace hook, lifted the lid of a saucepan to see if the mush was simmering, then turned to open the oven in the wall above the hearth. She slid her long paddle into the oven and lifted out two brown loaves of bread.

She smiled at Susan and Daniel, but did not stop working. An enormous amount of cooking and baking would have to be done that day to feed the eleven brickmakers and her own family and all the neighbors around Battenville who would come to help. Mrs. Anthony had been up since four; she would go on working until late that night. For everyone else this was a festive occasion, but Lucy Anthony already looked tired and harassed.

"Eat some bread and honey," she said. "You'll have to wait breakfast until the men get up." She shooed Daniel out, bread in hand, to get wood to keep her fire going. Straightening up a moment, Mrs. Anthony put her hand to her back and sighed.

Susan and her grandmother exchanged a sympathetic glance. The young girl and the old lady were much alike, both robust, both eagerly looking forward to all the work and the bustle and excitement of the day. They loved doing things, and being busy and active and taking charge.

Grandmother Read had managed a large farm in Adams, Massachusetts, raised seven children and had given them some schooling. The farm was now sold and would provide a good inheritance someday for her children. And she had done all this without much help from Grandfather Read. He had sat around and talked politics while she had done the work. Hard work it had been, too, but she was proud that she could do it.

Susan took after her, but her own daughter, Lucy, worked out of a sense of duty, without enjoyment. Young as she was, Susan felt sorry for her mother, although the world would consider Mrs. Anthony fortunate.

She was married to an up-and-coming, hard-working, intelligent man, very respected in the community, and Mrs. Anthony's lot in life was no harder than any other small-town housewife with children. Daniel Anthony even provided hired girls for her sometimes, but the family were Quakers and were used to "plain living." Now that Guelma, Susan, Hannah and Daniel were old enough to help their mother, the Quakers would have considered Lucy Anthony an idle woman if she couldn't manage her own household herself.

And Mrs. Anthony never complained. It was simply that she got so little fun out of work, Susan and her grandmother felt.

Susan, though, was brimming over with joy at the prospect of a busy day. She was put to work rolling out pie dough, and she considered this an honor. With a few expert hints from Grandmother Read she crumbled flour and rich butter together—moistened it just enough—then rolled it out into what would be a fine flaky crust. Then she began to peel apples for the filling.

The brickmakers came clattering down the stairs from their bedroom, hungry for their breakfast. No sooner were they seated when Daniel Anthony walked in to join them.

The moment he walked into the room everything and everyone brightened, but at the same time everyone unconsciously put on better manners. Even the brickmakers stopped gulping their food, straightened in their chairs and returned his kindly greeting with a "Good day to you, too, Friend Anthony."

He had a smile for his wife, which she returned. He teased his eldest daughter, Guelma Penn, "Well, G. P., I see thee put rag curls in thy hair last night. Shall I tell the Friends at Meeting how frivolous thou has become?" When she blushed prettily he patted her cheek and then Hannah's, but he stopped to speak to his favorite, Susan, and admire her pie. "If thee persists, child, thee may be as famous for thy pastries as both thy grandmothers." He kissed her. Susan adored him. Everyone respected and liked him, as well they should, for he was an unusual man.

He had built his first small cotton mill in Adams, Massachusetts, with his own two hands. It was too small, however, and he had moved to nearby Battenville, where he entered into partnership with Judge McLean, who put up some money while Daniel Anthony contributed his skill. Now he had a larger mill and fine prospects.

Daniel Anthony also had firm principles. Hating slavery, he would buy no raw cotton from the big Southern plantations that had slave labor. It cost more, but he sought out small independent farmers who worked their own cotton fields.

He had other strange ideas. He had a passionate faith in education for everyone, male or female, and every evening he conducted a class to which anyone in the small town of Battenville could come. What pleased him most was that the young women and men who worked in his mill came regularly, even after a ten- or twelve-hour working day.

Those working hours were shorter than what some other mill owners demanded. In 1832 it was nothing for an employer to expect his workers to put in fourteen hours a day, live in company shacks for which they paid the employer a high rent and buy their supplies at his store. In this way they were always in debt to their employer. Daniel Anthony would have none of this.

The women and young men who came off the farms and worked for Daniel Anthony were treated well. The women lived together in houses he had built for them, with small garden plots where they could grow their own vegetables and with hen houses for their chickens.

Now Mr. Anthony ate his breakfast quickly and hurried out with his son and the brickmakers, anxious to get to work on the final polishing, painting and varnishing of the new house. It was the symbol of his success. He had a modest pride in it.

With his going the kitchen settled down to an orderly fever of cooking. "Susan, we may need more eggs," said her mother, inspecting the larder with a worried air. "Run over to the mill and ask the girls if they can loan us a dozen." Mrs. Anthony did not use the "thee" and "thou" of the Quakers. She had been born a Baptist, and while she had become a Quaker and wore the simple Quaker grey dresses, their language was not natural to her.

Susan was fascinated by the mill—the hum of the spindles and the clack of the looms—and she was fascinated by the girls and men so industriously working at them. As usual, she sought out Sally Ann Hyatt. Whenever anyone wanted to know anything they looked for Sally Ann. In fact, just as Susan came in, the foreman called the mill girl over to ask what he should do about a loom that was not working properly, and she soon put it right. She was the most capable person in the mill.

When Susan asked for eggs, Sally Ann said that there were plenty in the house she shared with some other girls. She handed Susan the key and told her to help herself.

"Are all the girls coming to the party at the new house tonight?" asked Susan.

Sally Ann's face clouded. "I thought so, but I don't know. Molly says she has a toothache. I think it is only that she has nothing but her patched dress to wear. Her father comes every week to claim her wages and she has nothing for a party. Never mind, Susan," Sally Ann said, seeing the girl's distressed face, "we will find something for her."

"Can he do that, Mother?" Susan asked ten minutes later when she came into the kitchen with her apron full of eggs. "Can he take the money she earns?" Mrs. Anthony answered absentmindedly. "Poor thing." She was cutting up meat for stew. "Of course he has the right, but she should have a new dress once a year. Perhaps Daniel can talk to the man."

"The law," Grandfather Read stated, peering over his spectacles, "gives the father the right to do what he has done; the girl has nothing to say in the matter." Grandfather had come downstairs at last and had usurped his wife's rocker and now was contentedly reading his newspaper. "Daniel must not tamper with the law. Females are not fit to handle money; they would only spend it on frivolities. Fathers and husbands have the duty to protect their womenfolk from their follies. It is for females to obey. Such is their nature, poor sweet creatures." And he went back to his reading and rocking.

Susan looked at him and then at Grandmother Read, and it came to her, forcibly, that there was something very wrong with Grandfather's arguments. Elderly as she was, Grandmother was on her feet, standing at the kitchen table, still working, cutting out doughnut dough, while her husband did nothing. "Poor sweet creatures!" Was that what he thought of his wife?

"Susan, thee is paying no heed to what thee is doing," said Guelma. "There is no top crust to thy apple pie." Susan came back to her work, banishing every other thought. There was no time to dawdle. Wagons were arriving. Neighbors were coming to lend a hand for the last day's final work on the new house. There would be a host of hungry men to feed for the noon dinner and the evening supper.

The pies went into the oven. Five dozen doughnuts were already deep-fried and heaped up on platters, keeping warm on the hearth and waiting to be sugared. Great kettles of rich stew simmered, hanging on one side of the fire; another kettle of chicken pieces swung on a chain on the other side, sending out a rich, tantalizing aroma. A side of beef turned on the spit, roasting slowly.

Except for baby Eliza in her cradle, every female pair of hands was busy. Even five-year-old Mary helped by running errands, filling sugar bowls and salt shakers and carrying grain outside to feed the chickens. The usual household work had to be done as well as the extra cooking and baking. Beds had to be made, floors swept, dishes washed and dried, water carried, pail after pail, from the outdoor pump and wood brought in to keep the fire going.

Extra doughnuts, puddings, pies and cakes had to be made for the evening party. Quakers never had dancing parties, and Daniel Anthony would not permit any form of alcohol to be drunk; nevertheless, everyone wanted to come to an Anthony party. The older people came to talk to Daniel Anthony and listen to him, since he was a man of education, and since he had to travel to big cities to get contracts for his cotton, and there was so much he could tell them. The younger people played simple games and ate. The food was so good no one minded not having a dance or a drink.

This was unusual. It was an era of extremely heavy drinking. Rich people consumed a great many bottles of wine and brandy with every meal; poor people forgot they were poor and miserable by getting drunk on cheap gin; middle class people drank a lot of hard cider, beer and ale. Other Quakers drank, but Daniel Anthony was against it. He had seen too much misery caused by alcohol.

If a man came to work drunk and incapable of doing his job, he had to be fired; then his family suffered. Sick people died because the doctors were not fit to do their jobs. Husbands ill-treated their wives, and fathers their children. When Mr. Anthony moved his family from Adams to Battenville and built his mill and workers' houses and a bridge, the tavern-keeper complained he could hardly make a living, so few people came to drink in his place.

All day long Susan was too busy to visit the new house, but finally both dinner and supper were finished and everything was ready for the party. Then, in her sober, grey Quaker frock, her hair hanging straight down her back, she walked with her mother and sisters and her brother to the lovely, two-story house, so newly finished that the smell of paint and varnish still hung around some of the rooms. Along with the guests, who were a mixture of solid, well-to-do Battenville and Easton businessmen and their wives, farmers and farm hands, housewives and mill girls, they admired the large entrance hall with its curving stairway and the four fireplaces —kitchen, sitting room and bedrooms—and the carved and painted woodwork.

For a little while Susan enjoyed herself. Even after such a day she wasn't tired. She was a strong child, with broad shoulders, a straight back and a slim waist. She would have liked to join in the games but she was too young for those that needed partners. Guelma wasn't. She and young Aaron McLean, the son of Judge McLean, Daniel Anthony's business partner, joined hands when the others did.

In fact, Susan decided, she was too young to sit in with the grown-ups in the parlor and too young to join in most of the games, but she was too old to be put to bed, like Mary. She was in-between. The evening party fell flat and dull for her. She wandered around for a while and then went back to the old house, where Grandmother Read sat beside the sleeping baby in the cradle, and Grandfather pored over his newspaper by the oil lamp.

15

SUSAN B. ANTHONY

Susan sat on a footstool and rested her head against his knee. "What is in the newspaper, Grandfather?" she asked.

"Arguments about slavery, Susan. The Southern plantation owners claim they must have slaves, but there is an editorial condemning slavery as an evil, inhuman treatment of one race by another. Signed 'An Abolitionist.' Quotes from William Lloyd Garrison's newspaper, the *Liberator*. Boston man, Garrison is. He was told to shut up talking about slavery and you know what he said? Said: 'I will not equivocate. I will not excuse. I will not retreat a single inch—*and I will be heard!*' " Grandfather loved to talk and argue, but he laid down his paper and looked at Susan. "You don't care about such things. Females never do know anything about politics or economics or theology. Why aren't you at the party?"

"When I was your age, how I loved to dance!" sighed Grandmother Read.

"But you weren't a Quaker, Grandmother, and I am. I'm not allowed to dance. Besides, I like to listen to what the newspapers say. Quakers think females should have education and think and speak for themselves. My Grandmother Anthony, in Adams, and my great-grandmother both attained the High Seat in Quaker councils, but their husbands did not. That meant the Society of Friends considered the women smarter than their husbands. Father told me that," said Susan.

"Humph," her grandfather snorted. "Quakers are good people, but it isn't in nature for a wife to be set above her husband. Isn't in the Bible, either. Women are put on earth to obey and please men and keep their mouths shut. It's up to men to run the world and protect the women." Susan was sure she saw a wink in Grandmother Read's eye. Perhaps Grandfather saw it, too.

He rattled his paper angrily and changed the subject. "Article here about people moving out West, heading for the other side of the Mississippi. Going to be trouble with Indians. Going to be trouble, too, in Washington. Are they going to be slave states or free? There'll be fights. Maybe the whole nation'll be caught up in it. Civil war."

This was beyond Susan's understanding. She yawned and rested her head on her grandfather's knee but she did not doze. Something was bothering her. "Grandfather, tell me —when Sally Ann knows more about the mill than anyone else, why isn't she foreman? Even he has to come and ask her advice about everything. She knows more than he does."

Mr. Read slammed the newspaper against the rocker arm. "What nonsense do you have in your head? What a silly . . ." He checked himself, looking upward. Susan felt a strong hand reach under her chin and tilt her face, and her eyes met her father's. His were not angry, like Grandfather's, but deeply troubled.

He said softly, "I have often thought the same, daughter, because Sally Ann deserves the job and the money. But it would not do. The men would quit. So would most of the girls. They would not work for her. It is wrong, but that is how it is. Now!" His face lightened and his eyes smiled. "Guess what I am eating?" He held out a plate. "The best dish of the whole party—thy own apple pie!"

The day bloomed for Susan again. What did it matter if she was in-between ages or not as pretty as Guelma? She was loved and appreciated. She was, also, suddenly very sleepy. She felt herself lifted and carried upstairs to her old room, to sleep there for the last time.

The next day, while she helped move the last furnishings,

17

she thought sometimes about how men felt about women and girls. It didn't really seem fair. Yet she, herself, was a lucky girl, and by the time evening had come she had put the whole problem out of her mind.

The next few years in the new house saw many events: some wonderful, some terrible. On April 19, 1834, the Anthonys' second son, Jacob Merritt—always called Merritt —was born, but a month later little Eliza, aged two years, died. Mrs. Anthony was grief-stricken. The care of the household fell upon Susan and Guelma, with the help of their younger sisters and brother.

Grandfather and Grandmother Read also died, but their passing was peaceful. They had lived long, full lives and Mrs. Anthony felt regret but no tearing agony at such deaths.

Mrs. Anthony eventually recovered her health, and the two older girls were able to give more time to their studies. Their father's business was prospering so that he could plan higher education for them. There was a great demand for cotton, and he and Judge McLean expanded their mill, borrowing money to do so.

Although he was in debt, the prospects were so good, Mr. Anthony was able to send Guelma to Deborah Moulson's Quaker finishing school near Philadelphia. In the fall of 1837 Susan joined her sister there. She was thrilled at the prospect of a valuable education. Very few girls in 1837 had any schooling beyond reading and writing. But the months she spent there turned out to be some of the most miserable in Susan's life.

Deborah Moulson set a high standard of scholarship and offered excellent classes in English, Orthography, Reading,

Writing, Arithmetic, Grammar, Geography with the use of maps and globes, the elements of Astronomy, Natural Philosophy, Chemistry, History and Composition. At first Susan flung herself with joy into her classes.

She found that nothing she could do would please the headmistress. Deborah Moulson was an ill woman and her illness made her a tyrant. Pupils like Susan felt the full weight of her wrath, while those like Guelma escaped. Once Susan was goaded into exclaiming: "It is not fair! Guelma is thy favorite. She can do nothing wrong and I can do nothing right, no matter how hard I try."

"Thy sister Guelma does the best she is capable of," replied Miss Moulson. "Thee has greater possibilities so I demand more of thee."

Susan was astounded to be told she was more intelligent than her sister. She had no false pride and knew she was neither quick-minded nor brilliant; she had to work doggedly hard to learn.

It was this persistence her teacher saw, and the reason why she drove her so relentlessly. The girl strove and struggled, yet she could never seem to please, and her diary was blotted with her tears.

She wrote: "2nd month, 12th day. Deborah came down in the afternoon to examine our writing. I offered mine for her to examine. She took it and pointed out some of the best words as those which were not well written and then asked me the rule for dotting the i, and I acknowledged I did not know."

At this point the teacher had loudly exclaimed to the whole class that it was no wonder she suffered so much from illness when she tried so hard to teach Susan and was so ill-rewarded. Susan had dashed out of the room, run upstairs and had thrown herself on her bed to cry her heart out before once again writing out another failure in her diary.

It was with relief, then, that Susan received a letter from her father. He was coming to take her and Guelma home. At the time she did not stop to wonder at this sudden change in plans. She was only overwhelmed with joy at escaping from Deborah Moulson.

But when her father did come she was shocked to see the terrible change in Daniel Anthony's face. Distress and worry had etched lines around his eyes, and his mouth was set in a bitterness the two girls had never seen before. Neither of them understood the world of finance and business. They were bewildered as he tried to explain it to them during the long journey home.

All America was in the grip of a financial crisis and panic. Banks, businesses, mills and factories were closing down. Retail stores were afraid to buy. Before Daniel Anthony had come to take the girls home he had gone to New York and called upon one buyer after another—the people who usually wanted his fine woven cotton. Not one would make a purchase or a contract. Many of these houses had closed their doors.

What was he to do? His mills were heavily mortgaged. He had come to Battenville, originally, on the urging of Judge McLean, who had seen what a good, small mill Daniel Anthony had built in Adams. Judge McLean had a much larger building in Battenville and there was much greater water-power there; he would donate the building and put up the money to get started, and Mr. Anthony would put in his skill to run it, as his share of the bargain.

They had started small, but in order to compete with

other mills they had to expand and put up more buildings and buy more machinery, and they had to do this on credit. Now bankers held the mortgages; if Daniel could not pay the interest they would take the mills and every cent the family had.

The bankers reminded Daniel that if he had not been so stubborn he might have bought his raw materials more cheaply and not be in such danger. To this the Quaker turned a deaf ear. He had refused—and always would—to buy his cotton from farms or plantations worked by slave labor. To have done so would have been to condone a slavery he hated.

With the girls at home he struggled on for nearly a year. The mills weren't paying so he opened and ran a paying school, instead of the free one he used to conduct in the evenings. Susan taught nearby at Union Village. She and Guelma saved every penny to give to their father. It was all of no use.

The end came slowly but inevitably. The mills closed down. The girls and men went back to their farms. The creditors closed in. They would take the mills and the lovely brick house. That was only fair. What seemed cruel to Susan was that they demanded *everything* in Battenville —everything the family possessed.

There was to be an auction. In a daze Mrs. Anthony and Susan wandered through all the rooms and saw that the auctioneer had already laid out and labelled for the inspection of possible buyers such items as "one baby's cradle," "twelve silver spoons," "family Bible," "large dictionary," "boys' pocketknives," "coffee grinder," "pewter porringers" and "copper kettles." All of her mother's wedding presents had to be sold. Almost every dress and coat and cape which the parents and children were not wearing on their backs had to go. Even the eyeglasses of both father and mother were laid out on a table for sale, and the worn schoolbooks, also.

Through a mist of tears Susan saw Grandmother Read's rocking chair labeled for sale. She touched it gently and as she did so, she remembered. The Reads had left all their children—sons and daughters—a share in the sale of their big farm. Where was Lucy Anthony's inheritance? Couldn't that save them?

It must be that Uncle Joshua, Lucy Anthony's brother, had it in his possession. Why couldn't they write to him? Why couldn't he . . . ?

Suddenly, behind her, the door opened. She turned and saw a portly, distinguished-looking, well-dressed gentleman.

"Uncle Joshua!" she cried, and hurled herself into his arms. "You'll save us, won't you?"

He patted her shoulder. "We'll see," he said.

Chapter Two

At the auction Uncle Joshua bought back all the sentimental, important personal possessions for the family, but he would not give one cent to save the mills or the house. He was too shrewd a businessman for that. If Daniel Anthony did not lose them this year, he would lose them the next.

He greatly admired Susan's father for his brains and abilities. But he knew that the way to survive a business panic was to cut wages, force the workers to labor longer and harder, sell them their food and keep them in debt. Daniel Anthony was too fair and kind a man to compete with other mill owners. He did not have enough capital or meanness to succeed.

Lucy Anthony's inheritance was in Joshua's care and Daniel agreed to this. Otherwise the husband's creditors could have seized the wife's property to pay the husband's debts. This was the law.

Married women had no right over an inheritance; it passed directly into their husband's hands. Wives also had no authority over their children; the husband decided everything. If a wife worked, her salary was not hers; if she ran a shop it was legally his; if she left her husband because he was a brute she went out penniless. Daniel Anthony kept quiet about Lucy's inheritance because he thought the law unfair, while Uncle Joshua kept quiet to conceal the money. When and if he approved of his brother-in-law's plans he would surrender it to him, but not before.

Joshua understood that his brother-in-law had to try to do things his own way. Uncle Joshua went back to Palatine Bridge, in New York state. There, in the twin towns of Palatine and Canajoharie, he waited like a benevolent spider in his web of banks, stage lines, hotels and turnpike toll houses, which he either owned or had an interest in, for Daniel Anthony to come to him for advice and money. He understood the fierce pride that would make Daniel try everything else first.

All this Susan began to understand, little by little. It was the first understanding she had that goodness and brains did not always win, but it was not her first shock of understanding that women had no rights over their own inheritances and were considered "inferior" people.

She had seen that in the mill, when a girl could not be made foreman. She had seen fathers and brothers come and demand the mill girls' salary—with Daniel Anthony powerless to prevent them. Now she saw that her mother's money was not really hers at all. Men had charge of it. But because Daniel Anthony had respect for women, he did not demand his wife's money. He would succeed, on his own.

Uncle Joshua did not approve of Daniel's next move, but he said nothing. Three miles away, in the small town of Hardscrabble, Daniel Anthony owned a small satinet mill, a grist mill and a lot of timberland. Actually, all of this was mortgaged, too, but to different creditors who were not yet pressing him for payment, and here Daniel hoped to re-build his fortune and make the mills pay. He moved his family early in 1839.

Their new home had formerly been a tavern and was quite large. It had none of the elegance of the brick home they had lost, but it was comfortable. It even had a third story which was all one big room and had formerly been used for dances. The house would have been comfortable if the Anthonys had not been so close to absolute poverty. They suffered cold in the freezing winters because they could not afford to have workmen fix the roof and walls which had holes in them. The fireplace could not warm rooms where there were such draughts of wind whistling through them.

Oddly enough, the Anthonys were not really unhappy. None of their old friends looked down upon them. Aaron McLean, whose father was also struggling to keep going in the financial crisis, drove over every chance he could to see Guelma. There were beaux for Susan and Hannah, also, though Susan had no special romantic feelings for any of the young men who came to take her on picnics or sleigh rides.

She was not as pretty as her two sisters, but she had per-sonality. Even Aaron, in a big brother way, liked to talk and argue with her because she spoke her mind and wasn't silly. Tall and slim, with her head always erect, she walked briskly. The vitality in her triumphed over her grey dresses and the prim way she had to wear her hair, parted in the middle and pulled back into a bun.

The young people of Hardscrabble came to Mr. Anthony and begged him to let them hold dances in the third story of his house, as they used to do when it was a tavern. If he would not allow this then they would have to go to a real tavern, where the innkeeper was only too glad to have them come so he could sell them liquor.

Daniel Anthony's conscience was torn. Quakers were not supposed to hold dances. Yet it would be worse, he felt, to expose all these young people to an unscrupulous innkeeper who would do everything he could to get them to drink. Mr. Anthony finally decided the Quaker rules must be set aside this once. The dances were held in his house.

Naturally, the Anthony girls could not dance. They had to sit along the wall and watch, which was torture. No matter how hard she tried not to, Susan's foot would jiggle and her eyes grow bright with the music, and she longed with all her vigorous nature to be prancing in the reels and polkas.

Since the family denied themselves the right to dance, it came as a blow when the local Society of Friends disowned Mr. Anthony for his action. The notice read:

> It is with great sorrow that we have to disown Friend Anthony, for he had been one of the most exemplary members of the Society, but we can not condone such an offense as allowing a dancing school in his house.

Daniel Anthony was hurt, yet he would not go back on his promise to the young people. He had acted according to his own wisdom and conscience and he would stick by it.

The "disowning" did not mean he and the family were no longer Quakers. They could still go to Meetings, but they had to leave when the business sessions began. They were slightly in disgrace.

To Susan it was all so unfair that, unconsciously, her strong, deep, ancestral ties began to loosen. She would always, to the end of her life, call herself a Quaker, but she had begun to cast off many of the rules and inhibitions.

All of this turmoil—the fun of the dances and the trouble arising out of it—was important at the moment of happening, but it did not amount to much against the desperate struggle of the family to keep going financially. No matter how hard he worked, Daniel Anthony was not prospering. His small mills could not compete with big ones. Yet he had to meet the payments on his mortgages. Guelma got a job teaching so she could bring him a little money.

Then it was Susan's turn. She was already doing most of the housework, baking twenty-one loaves of bread one day, doing a huge washing the next day, weaving carpets and making rag rugs, putting up curtains, spinning and cooking and sewing, but none of this earned a penny. She had to turn to the only profession open to women—teaching.

First she went to New Rochelle, where she was to be assistant teacher in a Quaker school. Miss Kenyon, the headmistress, became ill, and all the work fell on Susan's shoulders, in addition to nursing her employer. She did this for fifteen weeks, until Miss Kenyon was back on her feet again, and then Susan came back to Hardscrabble, in time for Guelma's wedding to Aaron McLean, on September 19, 1839.

Susan rejoiced over her sister's happiness. She liked her new brother-in-law and in spite of their different ideas, they were close. He had always written to her when she was away, just as he had to Guelma, except that she was more apt to get scoldings than affection.

She had written him from New Rochelle that she thought it shameful that three black girls, Quakers, were not allowed to sit even on the back seat at Meeting. "One long-faced elder dusted off a seat in the gallery and told them to sit

27

there," wrote Susan indignantly. She had gone on to say that she had made friends with the girls, invited them for tea and found them cultured and educated and delightful. Aaron was scandalized. He wrote back that he hoped the people of New Rochelle didn't think everyone in the Anthony and McLean families would behave as Susan did.

With Guelma gone to follow her husband in his career as a young merchant, Susan became the eldest child at home and she felt the responsibility. Money was so scarce that her father had taken on the extra job of postmaster when Hardscrabble changed its name to Center Falls. Susan wanted to stay close to help out at home, but also desired to earn some money, so she was glad to get the job of teaching at the local school. She was offered $2.50 a month to take the place of the male teacher who had been paid $10.00 a month when he quit.

The moment she walked into her new classroom she knew why the other teacher had quit. At the back of the room, lolling in their seats or perched on the desks, was a group of older boys. They were of school age but big and strong and tough and ready to put any teacher down. Susan was going to have to fight to keep her job.

When she walked in, wearing a grey dress with a white collar and an old silk bonnet, she knew very well that she appeared to them a mild and timid lady. They snickered. They looked at each other and laughed. One boy got up and stretched to his full size, flexed his muscles, stared at her as she walked to the front of the room and said loudly: "Looka the new teacher! Reckon she'll stay till noon?"

Susan could pretend to ignore this remark, but the Anthony pride burned like fire inside her. Little did the boys know how well the grey sleeves of her dress disguised the strong muscles developed from carrying logs of wood for the fire and buckets of water from the well, from churning, lifting, carrying, fetching, weaving and spinning. Little did they know the strength of will she had inherited from her father. She took off her bonnet and smoothed her hair.

"Good morning, class. Boys and girls, thee will all rise. I will read off thy names and thee will answer and then take thy seat to which I will direct thee. Gerald Andrews?"

The Quaker plain language was a new stunt and a source of crude laughter and jokes to the bullies in the back of the room. They howled with laughter. "Gerald," one of them mimicked Susan, "take thee seat. Dost thee not hear? Answer thee name." His friends pounded each other on the back with glee.

Susan paid no attention but looked at the younger children and repeated her request. A scared small boy piped up: "I'm Gerald Andrews, Miss."

Susan smiled at him, ignoring the tormentors in the back of the room, and motioned to him to come and take a front row seat in the right-hand section of the room. "This will be thy place from now on, and others of thy age will sit with thee."

He scuttled into his place. The bullies taunted him. "Do what teacher tells you to, you coward, but wait till we get thee outside. We'll learn you something she can't!!"

The next four names were of girls and they took their new seats obediently, and the boys only made slight fun of them. But the next name was Marcus Lutz.

"Marcus? Thee will go to the left side of the room, the second row."

"Try and make me. I like it right where I am. And if I don't like this place I'd jest as soon take your'n." He was the biggest and meanest of the boys. He was the ringleader.

Susan rose from her desk at the front of the room and walked slowly down the aisle to where he sat. Most of her attention was on him, sizing him up and seeing he was nearly as tall as she was and his fists were like hams. But in the back of her mind, almost unconsciously, she marveled that she was not afraid. Her knees did not tremble. Her hands did not shake.

Her heart was pounding, but she knew it did not show in her face. She had to present a picture of confidence and composure, come what may. She came to Marcus' desk and stood over him, and said in the mildest voice she could command:

"Will thee move to thy proper place, Marcus? Thee must do as I tell thee."

He sprawled back in his seat. "Try and make me. I'm likin' it, just where I am."

"I shall ask thee once more to move. We have much to learn in this classroom, and politeness and obedience must be learned along with reading and writing," she said. "Well, Marcus?"

"Maybe," he laughed, "you can teach the babies, but . . ."

He was not allowed to finish. Quick as forked lightning Susan's one hand fastened itself in his thick, matted hair, and the other grabbed the front of his shirt. She yanked him deftly from behind the desk and onto his feet, twisted him around and marched him down the aisle in front of her by shifting her right hand from the front of his shirt to the back of his neck. He howled. His hair was being pulled so unmercifully that he had to bend his head back. Tears were in his eyes.

He tried to fight back. He flailed his arms around and

tried to grab her, but Susan ordered him, "Keep thy hands still or I will pull thy hair out!" and he knew she meant it. While the rest of the school watched in shock and fascination, she frog-marched him down the aisle and over to the exact seat where he belonged by age and alphabet. She pushed him into it and then let his hair go and ran to her own desk and grabbed the stick used as a pointer.

The true test was still to be endured. The moment he was released he would be after her.

She was right. His face crimson with fury and humiliation, he gave a bellow and lurched up to seize her. He lashed out at her with his fist, and she brought the cane down on his arm and took the battle away from him.

Without a second's pause she rained blows on his back and shoulders and arms and legs so fast that he could not use his superior strength against her, and so hard that he could only yell in pain and use his hands to try to protect himself. Inch by inch, foot by foot, she forced him back to his seat. Thoroughly thrashed and thoroughly cowed, blubbering and begging her to stop, he sank down and put his arms on his desk and his face down upon his arms.

Then she stopped. He was licked. All the fight was out of him. His friends, the other troublemakers, were frozen into silence, absolutely awed by what had happened.

Smoothing her hair with trembling fingers, Susan went to the front of the room and stood there for a second, until her heart slowed down and her breathing became more normal. Then she picked up her attendance book and quietly read out the next name and indicated the proper seat.

Meekly, every single person answered, and obediently each went to the new seat. In a very short time she had the school just as she wanted it, graduated from small children up to big ones, and had given out the lessons for the next day. Slates and schoolbooks were distributed. The smallest children began to struggle with their ABC's and Marcus and his age group worked at arithmetic.

She looked at Marcus, his face tear-streaked and dirt-smeared where he had wiped it with his sleeve, his red-rimmed eyes intent upon his slate and slate pencil, and knew that she had not won her victory by strength and quickness alone. He was stronger, physically. She had won by sheer determination. He had backed away from the force of her personality as much as from the stick. Marcus and his friends had run a male teacher out of the school. Yet women, thought Susan, were supposed to be the weaker sex!

For the next five years, while her father struggled to make his small mills pay, Susan taught wherever she could get a position, and gave nearly everything she earned to her family. No matter how hard he had to pinch pennies, Daniel Anthony was determined that his children should have more education than local schools could give them. Susan and Guelma had had their chance at Deborah Moulson's, and now Hannah was sent to the Young Ladies Academy in Canajoharie, where she could live with Uncle Joshua Read and his family, and have to pay only tuition.

There was also one year of a sudden spurt of prosperity when the small mills seemed to prosper, and in that year young Daniel was sent to the academy at Union Village.

Hannah finished school and got a job teaching. Only Mary and Merritt did not have the chance to go away, but they received a superior education through the teaching of their father, older sisters and brother. When they got teaching jobs they sent money home. Daniel Anthony never asked for this help. He kept a careful record of every penny contributed. Someday he would pay it all back.

But no matter how hard the whole family worked, it was finally not enough. After five years Mr. Anthony had to admit that the mills were failures. He sought out Uncle Joshua and discussed the problem with him, and suggested that he go back to being a farmer, as his father and grandfather had been before him.

Uncle Joshua approved, especially when he looked over the thirty-two acre farm Daniel Anthony had found on the outskirts of Rochester, New York. It was a long way from Center Falls and Adams and all their old friends, but a clean break with the past might be all to the good. Besides, the Erie Canal had just been opened, which would provide good transportation between the western part of the state and the large cities of the eastern part. Rochester was certain to grow. It was a fortunate choice.

Having approved, Uncle Joshua now gave over his sister's inheritance money for the purchase price of the farm. The Anthonys prepared to make the move.

Hannah had just married Eugene Mosher, a young merchant in Easton, and young Daniel was away clerking in a store, so Susan left her teaching job and came home to help. In two wagons full of household furnishings and food supplies, they left Center Falls, November 7, 1845, and arrived in Rochester a week later.

That winter was hard for the Anthonys. It was the wrong time of year to have to make such a move, but that could not be helped. They would have to wait for the vegetable garden and for the crops; in the meantime, mush and milk was the staple diet. Mrs. Anthony was ailing, so Susan took charge of the house. It was Mary's turn to begin a teaching career and send home whatever money she could.

Daniel Anthony showed Susan his account book. Every cent his children had given him was faithfully entered. Soon he would pay them back, a hundred times over. Indeed, this was the last time of poverty for the family. The next year Susan helped her father and Merritt plant and cultivate the fruit orchard and vegetable garden. She was strong and she loved the work, so Mr. Anthony could leave much of it to her, enabling him to look about for work that would bring in ready cash. He found it selling insurance for the New York Life Insurance company, and he was an immediate success at it.

He opened an office in Rochester, dividing his time between it and the farm, and prospered well at both. He would never become as rich a man as Uncle Joshua. He did not have that kind of shrewdness, but he did not care so long as his family lacked nothing they needed.

Now that the hard times were past, and her work and money were not so necessary, Susan had a chance to think of herself. What would she do? In 1845 she was twenty-five years old. She could be called an old maid, but there were still many men who wanted to marry her.

Most of them were widowers. They had married young. They had seen their young wives die in childbirth and were looking for a second wife. They were not looking so much for romance as they were for a strong and capable woman, such as Susan Anthony.

She turned them all down. Other people—even her mother —worried about her. Married women had a certain prominent position in society, while old maids were laughed at. Susan thought this ridiculous. She was herself, Susan Brownell

Anthony, and she felt she could only gain by marriage if she really fell in love.

One or two men had stirred her heart. There had been one evening of acute unhappiness, which she entered in her diary, when she had gone to a party with one escort while the man she really liked had taken another girl. Still, the next day she realized that her heart was not broken after all, and that she was not actually in love.

Perhaps she never would be.

In that case she wanted to be more than just the dutiful daughter staying home. With the solid prosperity of the Anthonys growing every month, she might be needed—but her father wanted her to have a chance beyond the farm.

At this moment an offer came from the Canajoharie Academy offering her the position of headmistress of the female department, at a fine salary of $125 a year. Of course Uncle Joshua, who was a trustee of the Academy, was responsible for the offer, but by now she deserved it and took it gladly.

The position was an excellent one, and Susan lived with her married cousin Margaret, who was Uncle Joshua's daughter, so she had lots of company and a busy social life. For once she could think of herself, spend every cent upon herself—and she did.

Uncle Joshua was not a Quaker. "Get rid of that grey dress and your plain ways and speech, Susan," he advised her. He was a man who knew the world and how it judged people. "The school trustees and the parents and your pupils will judge you on what they see of you. For your position you should be a woman of elegance."

To the end of her life Susan B. Anthony was to call herself a Quaker, but it was an inward faith only. She stopped saying "thee" and "thou." She went to dancing parties. She learned how to dress. Because she was slim and straight, she carried herself with poise and her new clothes did, indeed, look extremely elegant on her.

It was a new Susan who blossomed out in muslins and silks and merino. She also bought a fox fur muff and a lace shawl, hats and gaily-colored sashes. The Quaker in her would not let her go so far as to buy jewelry, but she wasn't above wearing a brooch or a necklace when her cousin offered to loan them.

She allowed herself to be put into stays—the tight corset that fashion demanded. When her cousin Margaret pulled her in and laced her up tight, her waist was even slimmer than before. She learned to sway a little when she walked.

Almost intoxicated with the novelty of dancing and singing parties and carriage rides and the company of people with lots of money to spend on theaters and amusements, Susan had a wonderful time for a while. The Reads and all their friends were predicting a good marriage for her, and it seemed quite likely.

At her first quarterly school examination, to which were invited trustees and parents and influential citizens, to come and listen to how well her pupils performed, she was the star of all eyes.

She was dressed in a new muslin gown, one of a purple and white and blue and brown plaid mixture, with two flounces around the skirt and puffs at shoulders and wrists; a white linen collar; new blue cloth shoes with patent leather heels and tips; and her cousin's slim gold watch suspended on a chain above her waist. Margaret braided Susan's brown hair and then wound the braids around a big shell comb high on her head, and had them *sewn* there, to make them stay.

"She won't be a teacher very long," one trustee confided to Joshua Read. "Some man will marry Miss Anthony, mark my words." And Uncle Joshua told her he had heard all sorts of compliments on how smart and attractive she was.

Perhaps if she had fallen in love with any of the men who came calling on her, her story would have been quite different. But she did not. Not one appealed to her as a husband.

The frivolity of her new life was fun at first, but gradually she wearied of it and then grew desperate about it. Daniel Anthony had taught her that everyone's life should have meaning. What was the meaning of endless hours planning new dresses? Of having tea with starchy matrons, who thought of nothing but how splendid were their houses? Of the constant talk of money, money, money among the men?

Teaching didn't completely satisfy her. Susan had to find something more to use up the energy of her hands and mind.

Even the one outside organization which she did belong to was a fashionable one. All Uncle Joshua's friends approved of Temperance societies. Preachers approved on moral grounds, and businessmen because they wanted their workmen to stay sober. So Susan joined the Daughters of Temperance, the female counterpart of the Sons of Temperance, and did some good work.

The one thing she discovered there was that, in comparison with others, she had an extraordinary sense of organizing. If a meeting had to be planned the other Daughters wrung their hands and worried how to do it. Susan planned it, got speakers, raised the money, advertised, got good crowds and new members, and once even made a speech.

SUSAN B. ANTHONY

It wasn't enough to fulfill her, however. Too many things about life in Canajoharie appalled her.

Joseph Caldwell, the husband of her cousin Margaret, was a selfish man. Because he was a man he had the legal and established right to have his own wishes considered first, so he ordered Margaret to do what he pleased and paid no attention to her needs and problems. He was the master. She had to obey.

Once he complained of having a headache. At that time Margaret was seriously ill. Sympathizing with him, she remarked that her head was hurting too. Joseph Caldwell replied with contempt: "Oh, mine is the real headache, genuine pain. Yours is a sort of natural consequence."

Consequence of what, Susan wondered indignantly. Of being a woman and frail? Then why didn't he help her when she tried to keep house and look after the children while she was so ill? She heard him tell other men how he protected and indulged his wife, but if dinner wasn't ready when he wanted it, he threw a tantrum. He liked to hear preachers give sermons on the frailty and spirituality of women and how men, being made superior by God, must look after these tender beings placed in their care.

Yet if a child cried in the house he blamed Margaret. No matter how sick she was he wanted his potatoes cooked just so, his clothes cleaned and laid out for him, his every whim catered to. Susan pitched in to help but it made her furious to have him give her smirking compliments and say the schoolteacher mustn't spoil her nice hands by scrubbing the baby's clothes. Let his wife do that.

"It wouldn't hurt that lazy beast to do a bit of the washing, himself," Susan grumbled.

Margaret grew worse and when she died, in 1848, Susan resigned. She had been in Canajoharie two years, growing more homesick every day. In August she went back to Rochester.

Chapter Three

The first evening at home, sitting out on the lawn with the family around her, Susan told them how selfishly Joseph had treated Margaret in her final illness. "You would think," she said, her eyes flashing, "that he was the one who was suffering. He acted positively injured that she should have died and left him with children. He'll marry very soon, you'll see!"

Daniel Anthony smiled at his indignant daughter. She had arrived dressed most elegantly in her white gown with the pink satin stripe and pink rosettes, but had quickly discarded them for an old calico dress. He liked her new poise and manners, but he was enormously pleased to find she was the same Susan underneath.

"Thee has never suffered the indignities which befall most females, Susan. Thee has grown up in a household which honors women. I count their intelligence as high as that of men. You will be interested to hear, therefore, of the wonderful woman's rights convention we attended here in Rochester. It was one of the most inspiring things I have ever been privileged to see and hear. This was the second convention. The first was held in July of this year in Seneca Falls. I promise you, that will be an historic date."

Susan smiled, not quite believing that it was so important. One thing she had heard almost as soon as she had arrived. A law had passed the legislature which enabled married women to hold inheritances in their own right. It was a glad moment when Daniel Anthony could register the farm in his wife's name. Her inheritance had bought it, she deserved it. This Susan agreed with—but a woman's rights convention?

"A pack of women getting together," she scoffed, "to feel sorry for themselves. Let every wife stand up to her husband. That's the way to do it." Susan knew she could stand up to any man. She had whipped the biggest boy in her school. Much as she had sympathized with Margaret, she had also felt impatient with her.

Quiet Lucy Anthony, usually so silent, contradicted her. "You do not know its importance, daughter." And Mary, now twenty-one, challenged her older sister. "Thee should have heard the ladies stand up on the platform and speak so eloquently, sister. There was the stately Lucretia Mott in her white lace cap, and Mrs. Elizabeth Cady Stanton—so pretty, with her dark hair and her pink cheeks—and both of them so brave." In her enthusiasm Mary sparkled. "They have issued a Declaration of Sentiments, declaring themselves men's equals." Susan was dumbfounded. "You are getting ahead of the times," was all she could think of to answer.

The talk turned to Sunday, which was the next day, and the guests who would be coming. Susan sat back and listened and looked at them all, happy to be home and even happier to see how well they looked. Daniel, Jr., was away working, but Merritt was helping on the farm, growing tall and handsome and showing signs of an intelligent, ardent nature. Her father and mother both had touches of grey in their hair, but their faces were peaceful. Mr. Anthony's insurance office was expanding; he had clients as far away as Syracuse. With financial security had come contentment in their personal lives, and time to concern themselves with significant outside political issues. Mary was teaching and loving it; she had inherited her father's love of the schoolroom.

Listening to them talk, Susan realized that although the farm was on the outskirts of Rochester the family was not isolated. On the contrary. The farm was a magnet that drew a large circle of friends to it, especially every Sunday.

At first the Anthonys had met Quakers. Then the Quakers had split into two factions; then had come still another split, over the issue of slavery.

The Anthonys and their closest friends were strong abolitionists. Slavery had to go, at whatever cost. Even the possibility of a war had to be faced; even the breaking of the law for the "higher law" of conscience. Other Quakers thought they were wrong. Feelings ran so high that the Anthonys went to a Unitarian church for a while, but eventually the anti-slavery people of all religions began to gather every Sunday at the Anthony farm. It was a kind of Meeting, a social get-together, and a weekly time for serious, subversive planning.

Many a runaway slave owed his underground escape route and shelter to the whispered arrangements made among the Sunday visitors at the Anthony farm.

Listening to all this, so stirring yet so taken for granted by the family, Susan regretted even more her frivolous past two years.

The next morning she got up and put on her simplest gown. Into a bottom bureau drawer went the fashionable corsets. On the top shelf of the closet she put away her best straw bonnet with the satin ribbons, wrapped in paper to keep dust off it. She would not be wearing it for a long time.

Downstairs, in the kitchen, she gloated over the fact that she was the first one up. Her hands itched to be cooking and baking. Once again, as when she was twelve, there would be guests for noonday dinner. She welcomed the work that lay ahead of her.

By the time Mrs. Anthony rose that morning she found the kitchen fire burning well, the bread dough kneaded and rising and some loaves already in the oven. Susan was at the table making the pastry for which she and her grandmother had been famous, and Merritt was coming in with another load of wood.

Brother and sister had already made a conspiracy. They would do everything they could to spare their mother's strength and their father's time. They would take over the house and the outdoor work as much as possible.

Besides, Susan loved doing what was only hard dutiful work to her mother. All morning long she tested herself, to see if the past two years in Canajoharie had ruined her fingers' deftness in making light, flaky doughnuts, and if she still remembered the bay leaf and the thyme for the stew. She remembered. Her fingers had not lost their touch.

"How many will come to Meeting, Mother?" she asked.

"We never know," answered Mrs. Anthony. "It is not a formal Society of Friends, Susan, and many come just to talk of politics or visit with each other. The Reverend Samuel May will be here, I know. He wrote he was driving from Syracuse to be here this Sunday. Then there will likely be the Posts and the de Garmos—but you will meet them all, when the time comes." She hurried out to the grassy yard, where Mary was putting cloths on long trestle tables, and had a conference with her over seating arrangements.

While making peach cobbler by the open kitchen window,

SUSAN B. ANTHONY

Susan heard them saying that if—by some great good fortune
—either Wendell Phillips or William Lloyd Garrison should
happen to be in Rochester that day, they must be seated where
everyone could hear them and ask them questions.

Just before twelve o'clock the first wagon arrived, and
Susan met Amy and Isaac Post. Merritt whispered to his
sister that it was well known the Post's house was a station
on the Underground Railway, and runaway slaves were hidden there regularly before making their way to Canada.

Next came a carriage with the Hallowells; after them the
de Garmos, and then others whose names Susan could not
remember at the time. The guests and the Anthonys moved
around, visiting and talking to each other. Susan and Mary
shooed their mother out of the kitchen so she might talk to
her friends.

At one o'clock there was a sudden stir in the yard. A
wagon drove up. Mary exclaimed: "It is Friend Willis and
wife, and they have brought Frederick Douglass and his
family!" She ran to the stable yard, while Susan followed
more slowly. She was staring rudely, and knew she was but
couldn't help herself. Even in Canajoharie the name of
Frederick Douglass was known, rousing people either to
admiration or to anger.

What a giant of a man! This was her first thought.
Frederick Douglass, the escaped slave and now the brilliant
editor of his own newspaper, the *North Star;* one of the great
leaders of the Abolition movement. He was as large in body
as he was in mind. He had massive shoulders and the height
to match them, and a fine big head crowned with a thick,
bushy mane.

While Mrs. Anthony lovingly greeted Mrs. Douglass, and
Mary took charge of the Douglass children, from nine-year-

old Lewis down to the toddlers, Daniel Anthony introduced Susan to their father. She murmured something, she did not know what, overawed by the keen, intelligent eyes in the dark face that towered above her. He bent over her hand and said, "Another fighter for freedom, Mr. Anthony? You contribute many sons and daughters to our cause."

"This one has been away, teaching, but she feels as we do, as we *all* do, Friend Douglass," said her father.

Susan recovered her wits enough to mind her manners. "I am so glad to have this honor of meeting you."

Frederick Douglass laughed. "If you are staying at home now, Miss Anthony, you will likely be seeing us often. Rochester is now our home, and this farm is our favorite gathering place. But if you speak of an 'honor' you must meet my wife, Anna."

Except in her own father, Susan had never heard a man speak with so much sincere respect of a woman. He put out his hand. The attractive, brown-skinned woman came up and he placed an arm around her shoulders.

"I could do nothing without her," he said to Susan. "Did you know, Miss Anthony, that while I was in England, speaking for the antislavery groups there, she made shoes and sold them, to support our children? I never knew until I came back."

Anna Douglass smiled at him, then other guests came to claim the Douglasses and lead them into the center of discussions. Susan went back to the kitchen, suddenly anxious for her cooking.

One pie was slightly burned. The rest were all right. Both Mrs. Anthony and Susan busied themselves with the last-minute details of the big dinner, moving back and forth from the kitchen to picnic tables with heaped-up bowls and platters, hot dishes and cold dishes. Their guests slowly came, still talking, to take their places. Susan insisted that her mother join them, but she, herself, would be kept busy serving.

While everyone ate they talked. Susan found it frustrating and tantalizing to hear snatches of conversations as she went back and forth, bringing out fresh supplies of hot biscuits, honey, pickles and preserves, and taking out the emptied platters of sliced roast pork, boiled beef and cabbage, creamed chicken.

"Did thee bring any copies of the *North Star* with thee, Friend Douglass?"

"A dozen or more, in the wagon . . ."

"And has Garrison come round to approving your editing a second antislavery paper? He wanted you to write for his *Liberator* and . . ."

Susan lost the rest of that exchange, and when she returned to the tables with her fresh peach cobbler and thick cream to pour on it, the company was deep in denouncing the Fugitive Slave Law which had been passed. Susan had heard nothing of it, so recently it had been passed, and she would have liked to have lingered to listen.

". . . monstrous that these slave-catchers should be permitted to come north, walk into anyone's home, seize runaway slaves and arrest their sympathizers!"

"The law makes us all accomplices of the slaveowners and . . ."

Susan went in and brought out more pastries.

". . . go to jail rather than turn over an escaped slave to them. To disobey a bad law is good citizenship, I say. And . . . ," someone was saying, when he was interrupted by Anna Douglass.

"Miss Anthony," said Mrs. Douglass, suddenly, "is this peach cobbler one of your making? It is delicious."

The other guests broke off their political talk long enough to compliment Susan upon her superb cooking and baking, and to compliment Mrs. Anthony on having such a talented daughter. Susan blushed with pleasure. She had enough inherited pride from both grandmothers to feel flattered and happy with the praise.

Her problem was that she wanted to be both Martha and Mary—to feel the satisfaction of providing well for the guests, but also wanting to sit at the feet of such intellectual and active people and listen and learn from them.

There was so much she did not know! Of course, she had heard of the Free Soil Party and the Missouri Compromise and all the other words and phrases being tossed back and forth across the table, but their actual importance was something Uncle Joshua and his friends did not consider fit subjects to discuss at dinner parties.

After the meal was over and the dishes washed Susan only had a little time to come and sit on the grass and listen to her parents' friends talk of the struggle against slavery. Most of the women, being Quakers, felt as free as the men did to enter into the discussions, even to argue and disagree over some small point, and the women were as involved as their husbands in helping slaves to escape.

Late in the afternoon all the guests were gone. Then Susan had a little time, until the evening chores, to open and read Frederick Douglass' *North Star*. That night she sat up late and read back copies of William Lloyd Garrison's *Liberator* and Horace Greeley's *New York Tribune,* to which her father subscribed. She found a copy of Frederick Douglass' own book, the *Narrative* of his life, and got through the first chapter before the work of the day caught up with her and she grew too sleepy to keep her eyes open.

The book fascinated her. Having met him and seen how cultured and poised he was, she had difficulty identifying him with a small black slave boy who was beaten because he could read and write and insisted on teaching other boys; who would not obey; who fought back. Wiser slaves cautioned him to wait and obey and watch for his chance. When it came he was a young man. He had already met Anna Murray, a free black woman, in Baltimore, and they had fallen in love.

His chance to escape had come. With the help of other black men he had dressed as a sailor, pretending to be going North to catch his ship in New York harbor, carrying false papers. In spite of several narrow escapes he entered New York, September 4, 1838, and was safe in a free state.

If the Fugitive Slave Law had been passed then, his master could have sent slave hunters after him and dragged him back, in whatever state they had found him.

Frederick Douglass was safe from them now only because British and American abolitionists had raised the money to buy his manumission, his freedom, from Hugh Auld, his old master. He was safe. He was secure—or he could have been.

He could have settled down and made a good living with his strength and skills and brains. He might even have tried to forget his childhood beatings and lashings. But he never forgot. He dedicated his life to helping other black men and women to escape; he pledged himself never to rest until all slaves were free, everywhere.

Wherever there was a meeting of abolitionists, either the Massachusetts Antislavery Society or the New England Antislavery Society, Frederick Douglass was on the platform, telling his story and reminding his listeners that their black brethren were being whipped, beaten and killed. Women were sold away from their husbands. Children were torn from the arms of their mothers and exhibited in slave markets for sale to the highest bidder.

Pro-slavery mobs in the North invaded his meetings, pelted him with rotten eggs and even waylaid him outside for a beating. Nothing could stop Douglass, any more than it could stop Wendell Phillips or William Lloyd Garrison.

Susan read and listened and wished there was some way she could help.

Just now there was not. She and her father agreed that she would run the farm, and thus enable him to extend his profitable insurance business to other towns and cities. She entered into the argument joyfully, finding great pleasure in doing farm work and housework, keeping physically busy.

The physical work, however, would never satisfy her active mind, and Daniel Anthony had never thought it would. He looked upon the next two years that she ran the farm as purely temporary, as a time of learning, until his Susan could find her true career.

She did some substitute teaching but it only convinced her that she was not the born teacher Mary was. Then she turned her attention to the Daughters of Temperance in Rochester and in a short time built up a tiny group into an astounding success, with a big membership and a healthy treasury. It was nothing for her to organize meetings and box suppers and picnics, attracting good speakers, new people and new money.

She met the Boston editor, William Lloyd Garrison, who was called by many the "father of the Abolitionist movement." From his own lips she heard him tell how, in 1835, he had found a mob surrounding a meeting hall of the

Boston Female Antislavery Society. The ladies, escorted by police, had gotten away safely, but Garrison had been dragged through the streets at the end of a rope while the crowd threatened to lynch him.

"That was no mob of ignorant immigrants, Miss Anthony," said Garrison, his eyes glinting behind the strong-lensed spectacles, "they were some of Boston's richest citizens. Business men who have dealings with Southern planters. Touch one of them in his pocketbook and he becomes a howling savage!"

Susan also met the handsome, aristocratic Wendell Phillips. People fawned upon him because of his family and social connections, but Susan didn't give a hoot whether his blood was blue or purple. She'd seen enough of snobbery in Canajoharie to cure her of any such nonsense. What she did admire about Phillips was his great gift of eloquence.

When he spoke of slavery he scalded her with fiery words; when he talked of the fight against it she wanted desperately to be part of it. But how?

The great speaking team of Abby Kelley Foster and her husband, Stephen Foster, came to Rochester for a meeting. Afterwards Abby was struck by Susan's capabilities and enthusiasm and tried to persuade her to go with them on their lecture tour.

"Me? Up there on the platform with you? That would be," declared Susan, "like putting a turnip in a rose bed."

Even when she had to speak briefly at the Daughters of Temperance, among ladies she knew well, she felt awkward and tongue-tied. She was not gifted that way.

What could she do, she wondered? Run a farm all the rest of her life? Organize box suppers for temperance groups?

Be that smart Miss Anthony?—an old maid, yes, but a smart one!—as people spoke about her?

In 1850 she went to Syracuse and then to Seneca Falls, New York, to hear William Lloyd Garrison at antislavery meetings. Susan's hostess in Seneca Falls was a woman with whom she had corresponded on temperance matters—a woman named Amelia Bloomer.

The first sight of that lady was a shock to Susan. Mrs. Bloomer was wearing "bloomers," as the newspapers and public called the style, after her. It was a skirt that came just below her knees, and below that her legs were clad in baggy trousers. In an age when to see a lady's ankle was highly immodest and tantalizing, these bloomers were scandalous. Amelia Bloomer had adopted the costume as a protest against the long skirts, the many petticoats, the hoops and stays of fashion.

She illustrated for Susan how easy it was to climb stairs in them and walk in them, especially across muddy or dusty streets, where long trailing skirts were a nuisance. Susan agreed, but she thought the outfit absolutely ugly and had no desire to wear such things.

She found it embarrassing when she and Amelia walked down the street after the meeting and a gang of boys followed them, yelling, "Lookit the woman in britches!" and "Her pants is fallin' down!"

As they turned a corner the two women came face to face with William Lloyd Garrison and George Thompson, who had been the speakers. Accompanying them was a small, pretty, plump woman, with short, dark ringlets curling around her lively, smiling face.

"It's Mrs. Elizabeth Cady Stanton," Amelia whispered.

SUSAN B. ANTHONY

"Oh, do introduce me!" begged Susan.

Before Mrs. Bloomer could do the honors, William Lloyd Garrison made the introduction. "This is Susan Brownell Anthony, the daughter of our devoted friends, Daniel and Lucy Anthony; a young woman whom, I am sure, will one day be helping us to organize."

There was no need for him to identify Mrs. Stanton. She was too well known. But as much impressed and pleased as Susan was to meet her, Mrs. Stanton also saw something in this new acquaintance to want to be Susan's friend.

Years later Mrs. Stanton wrote down her impressions:

Walking home with the speakers, who were my guests, we met Mrs. Bloomer with Miss Anthony, in the corner of the street waiting to greet us. There she stood with her good, earnest face and genial smile, dressed in grey delaine, hat, and all the same color, relieved by pale blue ribbons; the perfection of neatness and sobriety. I liked her thoroughly from the beginning.

A few weeks later Susan went to Seneca Falls to call upon her. She found Mrs. Stanton dressed in the "bloomer" costume and looking at herself distastefully in the mirror.

She saw the surprise on Susan's face and laughed. "Isn't it dreadful? I dislike it, but my husband insists I wear it. He says it is an expression of freedom for women, and of course he is right. It's actually much more comfortable than skirts that drag on the floor. The trousers give the legs much more freedom."

To prove it she gave a kick and then tried out a polka and went dancing around the room until she heard giggles from the doorway. "Oh, you children! Run away and play and don't come spying on your silly mother. Shoo!"

"How many children do you have?" asked Susan.

"Three, and I'm expecting another. I only hope it doesn't arrive just when I'm busy with the woman's rights convention. Well, I shall just have to go on the platform, anyway. You *are* interested in woman's rights, aren't you, Susan?"

Susan had never met anyone so merry and full of spirit as this new friend, but she shook her head regretfully. "I'm sorry. I think women should be equal, yes, but I can't get interested in something so unlikely to happen."

"We'll get there, step by step," replied Mrs. Stanton. "I wrote you asking you to come visit me because I thought you'd be a good one to advise us on a special project. I know you've been a teacher, so I've asked you here today to meet Horace Greeley, the editor, and Lucy Stone, and we'll put our heads together and see what we can do to promote coeducational schools."

To meet the editor of the *New York Tribune* and Lucy Stone was a thrilling invitation. Lucy Stone, a graduate of Oberlin College, had once protected the Reverend Samuel May from a mob who wanted to kill him because he was an Abolitionist. She had walked through the streets of Haverhill, Massachusetts, defying his attackers to touch him or her. Awed by such a courageous woman, the mob had fallen back and allowed them to go on.

Yet Susan was cautious. "I am in favor of opening all academies to girls, instead of only to boys, of course. But I must remind you, Mrs. Stanton, that I am not entirely in favor of woman suffrage. Why do you care so much about it?" Susan asked. "Why not spend our time fighting slavery?"

Then Mrs. Stanton told Susan her story.

She had been born into a well-to-do home; her father, Judge Cady, was a man of property and pride. He had given her an excellent education, seeing that she was tutored in both Greek and Latin, and then sending her to Emma Willard's Seminary in Troy, New York. Along with her classical studies, however, she had studied what was going on around her country and became a staunch advocate of the abolition of slavery.

This led to her meeting a poor lawyer, Henry Stanton, who was poor because he gave up his practice to become an agent for the American Antislavery Society. Against her father's opposition, Elizabeth married Stanton. The two went to London for the World Antislavery Convention.

There they found that women could not sit in the main hall but had to be quiet and listen, behind a screen, where they could not even be seen. William Lloyd Garrison was so incensed that he left the floor and went to sit with the women, while Henry Stanton made one of the most powerful speeches of the convention to condemn such outright discrimination by one group of abolitionists against another—men against women.

"And most of those hypocrites, Susan," said Mrs. Stanton, "were ministers of the gospel. They used the Bible to prove that women were subservient to men, should obey men and not try to sit as equals with men. Sanctimonious hypocrites! It was then that both my husband and I realized that the freedom of women from their bondage was as important a cause as was freeing Negroes from their slavery. Frederick Douglass agrees with us, bless him. After all, a Negro woman is doubly oppressed."

Mrs. Stanton had found Lucy Stone and Lucretia Mott in

agreement with her. The first woman's rights convention was sponsored by them in Seneca Falls, New York, in 1848.

"But don't we divide our efforts too much, Mrs. Stanton, when we try to work for every kind of emancipation at the same time?" asked Susan.

"That's why we need you! There is so much work for us, Susan!" entreated her new friend that day.

From the beginning, and for all their lives, they were "Susan" and "Mrs. Stanton" to each other. The married woman was six years older of the two; it was she who was the other's teacher, at first. Susan could not call her "Elizabeth." It simply was not natural to her.

In spite of the discussion that afternoon with Lucy Stone and Horace Greeley, nothing immediate came out of their plans for coeducational schools. Susan went home very thoughtful, however. Was she really needed? What could she do when she thought herself such a poor public speaker and when writing thoughts and ideas came so hard to her?

Susan was not ready for a big change. She would stay in her own backwater for a while longer: the temperance crusade.

In January, 1852, the Sons of Temperance held a large meeting in Albany, New York. Susan was sent by the Rochester Daughters of Temperance as a delegate. As she found a seat and looked about her she saw a large number of women delegates scattered throughout the audience.

The business meeting began. For a long time Susan listened. Then there came a point of business which was of interest to the Rochester society; without giving her action any thought she got to her feet to be recognized by the chairman.

"Mr. Chairman . . ." she began.

SUSAN B. ANTHONY

There was a hush over the entire room. This startled Susan, so she hastened to explain. "I am Susan B. Anthony, delegate from the Daughters in Rochester and I would like to express our feeling about . . ."

She got no further. The chairman came to the edge of the platform, looked sternly down at her and said: "The sisters are not invited here to speak, but to listen and to learn."

Shocked and furious at this outrageous public rebuke, Susan looked around her for support. Not a man would meet her eye and most of the women bent their heads. A few women did look at her and showed their sympathy. Susan turned and walked out of the building, and those few other brave ones got up and followed her.

"Listen and learn!" she exclaimed, as they gathered around her in a circle on the sidewalk. "Perhaps they could learn something from us! Our Daughters of Temperance in Rochester has tripled our membership; we are larger than the men's group, and we contributed more money to this mass meeting. All right, if we cannot speak in there, I suggest we hold our own meeting."

They all agreed. They followed Susan to the home of the clothing shop in Albany, run by the Quaker sisters Lydia and Abigail Mott. Susan had known them for a long time—ever since Lydia had been, for a brief time, an assistant teacher at Deborah Moulton's. Both sisters were noted for their cleverness, their independence and their ability to get along in a man's world by their own skills and wits.

The Mott sisters approved the walking-out and the separate meeting. They helped. They hired the lecture room of the Hudson Street Presbyterian Church, and sent Susan down to insert notices in the newspapers.

The evening of the meeting was cold. The church stove smoked and its chimney pipe fell down. Not many people came. Yet in spite of all the difficulties those who did attend were full of enthusiasm when Susan proposed that, instead of being a group attached to the superior men's group, they should form their own separate one: the Woman's State Temperance Society. The Reverend Samuel J. May was there and promised to persuade the women of Syracuse to join. So did David Wright of Auburn.

From this small handful of women grew a statewide organization, large and powerful, which Susan B. Anthony could take credit for. Many people helped her. Her father gladly encouraged her, hired a man to help at the farm and gave her whatever money she needed for her expenses. When it came time for the first state convention Horace Greeley published large notices of it in his *Tribune,* and Elizabeth Cady Stanton agreed to make the principal speech.

But it was Susan, overcoming her reluctance to put herself forward, who presided over the meeting and did so with the skill of a seasoned parliamentarian.

The Woman's State Temperance Society grew in size and such importance as to put the male group into the shade. Susan tried for an alliance. She was not antiman. The men steadfastly refused to let the women visit their meetings on any other basis than to "listen and learn."

In the same year of 1852 the New York State Teachers Association held its annual convention in Rochester. Susan saw the notice and read the rules: anyone who had taught or was teaching, and who paid a dollar, was entitled to attend with full rights. She paid her dollar.

When she entered the huge Corinthian Hall it did not surprise her to see that nearly two-thirds of the delegates were women. Teaching was one of the few honorable professions open to females; it was only natural that they should flock to it.

SUSAN B. ANTHONY

For two days Susan sat and listened. For two days she saw that the president and speakers on the platform were all men; any motion from the floor was made by a man. The women sat silent. It was not to be endured.

She wrote in her diary that second night: "My heart was filled with grief and indignation thus to see the minority, simply because they were men, presuming that, in them, was vested all wisdom and knowledge . . ."

On the next day the subject of the meeting was one of great interest to her: "Why the Profession of Teacher is Not as Much Respected as That of Lawyer, Doctor or Minister."

She knew why. After listening to the men debate and discuss this for several hours, she rose to her feet. "Mr. President!" she called out in a clear, penetrating voice.

Her words in her female voice injected a paralyzing horror into the meeting. The president, Charles Davies, professor of mathematics at West Point Military, dressed in resplendent military costume of blue coat and brass buttons, froze rigid for a long second. Then he leaned forward.

"What will the lady have?"

"I wish," said Susan composedly, "to speak to the question under discussion."

The president looked at the dignitaries seated on the platform. They looked wildly at each other and craned their necks to see this strange woman. The president finally stuttered: "What . . . what is the pleasure of the convention?"

One delegate shot to his feet. "I move she shall be heard!"

Susan's heart gave a great bound of joy. At least there was one man on her side. But other men were shouting: "Never! Make her sit down! For shame!"

"Let her speak!" came another call. The debate raged for a half hour and all that time Susan stood. Parliamentary procedure said that if she sat down she relinquished the floor to the next speaker. She stood.

Her endurance paid off. Unable to get rid of her, the request was finally put to all the male delegates to vote upon, and to her joy the majority voted yes. She had won.

So she told them why the profession of teacher was not as respected as that of lawyer, doctor or minister. Larger and larger numbers of women were teaching; as long as male teachers looked down upon women teachers as brainless, what would the outside world think of males who did the same work?

"Do you not see that so long as society says woman has not brains enough to be a doctor, lawyer or minister, but has plenty to be a teacher, every man of you who condescends to teach admits that he has no more brains than a woman?"

Her sarcasm made its point. She saw it in the red faces of the men on the platform; she heard it in the utter silence of the room. Now her legs were shaking so much she had to sit down.

The meeting went on in a very subdued fashion, but Susan B. Anthony listened to none of it. She was listening to her own heart and mind; inwardly she was hearing the voices of Mrs. Stanton and Lucy Stone and her own father.

All her doubts were swept away. She knew at last what her true cause was. Until women won their right to be equal, until they could reach their full potential as educated, free, active human beings, everything they would try to do would suffer. And until women reached their full potential, causes such as education and slavery would suffer. Men could not do it alone. From now on she was Susan B. Anthony, crusader for human rights—but especially for woman's rights.

Chapter Four

Susan cut her hair short and put on bloomers as her first act of independence. Then she sought out Mrs. Stanton again to tell her she had changed her mind. The older woman was delighted. "We'll get right to work!" she declared, pulling chairs up to her desk.

It was the first time these two women sat opposite each other, planning, putting forth ideas, getting together as a team—but it was by no means the last.

The first thing to be discussed was the big conventions to be held in September of 1853, in New York City. The first World's Fair was to be held there at that time and great crowds of people would be flocking there from all over, from north and south and from as far west as the territories of Kansas and Missouri. There might even be visitors from California and Texas! The gold rush in California had attracted thousands of Americans; the rich ones would surely make for New York's World's Fair.

Susan and Mrs. Stanton settled down to business. They had to help with the antislavery conventions and plan their own woman's rights convention. Almost as a sideline, Susan would put on a woman's temperance meeting.

At once the differences between the two women became evident. Mrs. Stanton had a quick, brilliant, sweeping mind that darted here and there, taking on such daring issues that Susan was astonished. Mrs. Stanton was just as willing to get up and speak on divorce, the stupidity of most religious leaders, clothes or anything else, as she was to speak on the vote for women or money rights for women. She could scribble notes that would make a wonderful speech or she could get up on a platform without notes and shock or charm an audience.

But if Susan was awed by her friend's brilliance, Mrs. Stanton was unable to believe that anyone could be so wonderfully practical as Susan. How could Susan *think* of all those little details? How could she remember them all?

To Susan, who had planned and cooked meals for twenty and thirty people, it was second nature. If you didn't plan ahead then the potatoes got overcooked while you tried to baste the roast; if you didn't remember the salt and the right amount of sugar and butter, you had a soggy, flat-tasting cake. Organizing a convention was much the same. You had to think of who would speak, what hall to rent, how much to pay for it, where the money would come from, how to advertise it, what you wanted to come out of it. You didn't wait until the last minute, as Mrs. Stanton was inclined to do. Everything had to be done well in advance, and everything in order.

The Stanton children—far from resenting this intruder in their household—loved Aunt Susan. Their own mother might forget what time they had their meals or came home from school, but Aunt Susan never did. And Henry Stanton looked upon her as a dear sister, the one who could make his tiny, charming wife toe the mark and get down to work.

SUSAN B. ANTHONY

September arrived in New York, and so did most of the antislavery and woman's rights people. Susan stayed with the Stantons but she was out from morning until night, with her hands full. There were going to be two temperance conventions: the Sons and the Daughters. There would be an antislavery convention and a woman's rights convention, and they all came one or two days after each other. The huge flock of World's Fair visitors, eager to be entertained, would likely drop in just to see what was happening.

The Woman's Temperance Society meetings came first, for which Susan was almost entirely responsible. The *New York Tribune* praised it highly. Their editorial stated: "This has been the most spirited and able meeting on behalf of temperance ever held."

The Men's Temperance Society put on a disgraceful exhibition. Miss Antoinette Brown, a lovely, young, intelligent preacher, was an accredited delegate but she was refused the right to speak. Susan was in the audience, furious that sanctimonious male preachers would get up to say that a woman preacher was "an abomination in the sight of the Lord."

Next came the Woman's Rights Convention at the Broadway Tabernacle. Lucretia Mott, the dignified president, convened the session and introduced the speakers: Mrs. William Lloyd Garrison, Wendell Phillips, Reverend William Henry Channing and Lucy Stone, among other prominent persons.

The great Tabernacle hall was full. It was wonderful to see so many people—especially so many men—in the meeting. At least it seemed wonderful, at first. Then it became apparent that a great many of the men were there to break up the convention if they possibly could.

At first they satisfied themselves with booing and catcalls,

SUSAN B. ANTHONY

but then they became bolder. The sight of the handsome, elegant Wendell Phillips standing on the platform beside the beautiful Lucretia Mott, in her sober Quaker grey, seemed to outrage the mob. The men hurled every kind of foul insult at the speakers. They stood up and shook their fists and threatened bodily harm to anyone brave enough to try to speak.

The convention leaders kept cool. They delivered their addresses even when they knew the audience could hear only a part of what they said. And when the official speeches were finished, brave women in the audience knew it was their turn to get up and face the bullies.

Not since Susan had handled her tormentor when she was teacher and he was pupil had she known physical fear. She knew it now, as she got to her feet. It seemed to her it would take little for this mob to get out of control and go smashing and trampling through the hall. Yet she must speak.

She told the convention of her experience at the teachers' mass meeting; she reminded the audience that a woman principal in Rochester earned $250 a year while a male principal doing the same job got $650 a year. As she talked she kept her voice clear and loud, trying to ignore the shouts from all sides of her.

"Git yourself a husband, you silly old maid!" someone was yelling, while others called to her to "Sit down!" "Shut up!" "Go back home where you belong!" One man, directly in front of her, knelt on his chair to face her and chanted, over and over, "Bow-wow, bow-wow, bow-wow" until she wanted to slap him across his rat-like face.

But she went on talking ". . . the Teachers Association has adopted a resolution to promote such action as will give women equal pay . . ."

SUSAN B. ANTHONY

"I'll pay you, I will! With this!" said a man getting out into the aisle and shaking his fist at her.

". . . for equal positions, and other tokens of equal respect," continued Susan. She had introduced herself by name when she rose to speak, and one very drunken man, who obviously thought the whole convention was a joke, kept jeering at her, "Go to it, Susan! Go to it, old girl!" and between that and the bow-wowing going on in front of her, and all the shouted profanities and insults, she could feel her knees begin to shake and her mouth tremble. But up on the platform stood Lucretia Mott, looking steadily and confidently at her, and Wendell Phillips smiling at her. Susan gathered strength from them and went on.

So did other women. The hecklers could not daunt them. The mob finally left when they found it was poor sport to try to frighten women who did not scare easily. On the second day of the convention only a few hecklers showed up.

Actually they succeeded in doing the opposite of what they hoped. Women like Susan B. Anthony became steeled against their attackers, while many new, timid women came forth to join the woman's rights movement.

Almost all the supporters of that convention turned up for the antislavery one; as far as Susan was concerned the cause was the same: freedom. The abolitionists had to face angrier hecklers and interrupters. The Fugitive Slave Law divided people right down the middle, with no more room for neutrals or moderates. The audience of supporters was greater than ever; Northerners were outraged that a South Carolina or Georgia slave hunter had the right to invade their states and drag away black men and women who should have been free under Northern laws. But there were also many who hated blacks and Abolitionists for stirring up trouble, as they claimed.

The meetings were riotous.

When the World's Fair was over Susan and Mrs. Stanton conferred upon the next steps. Mrs. Stanton was impetuous; she was all for campaigning for everything, for the vote, for divorce, for breaking into men's professions. Susan was more realistic. What women needed first was the right to have money. The 1848 law gave a married woman control of real estate or money inherited from parents, but what about money earned by both husband and wife—or just the wife?

"Woman must have a purse of her own" was Susan's argument, "and how can this be so long as the law denies to the wife all right to both individual and joint earnings?" She got the Reverend Samuel May to help her draw up a petition which set forth women's rights in regard to wages, the guardianship of children and the vote. Let divorce and other problems wait, she believed—to which Mrs. Stanton reluctantly agreed.

Back in Rochester Susan discussed her future with her father and mother. She wanted to get her petition printed in large numbers; she wanted to get thousands of signatures to the petition. It would take much of her time. The Anthonys agreed she should do what the cause demanded of her; it was she who insisted that she would only campaign in the winter time, when the summer and autumn harvest was gathered in at the farm.

The rest of the family was making changes, or thinking about them. Both Hannah and her husband, and Guelma and Aaron McLean had moved to Rochester, but even as the family circle tightened in this way it loosened in another.

SUSAN B. ANTHONY

Young Daniel was already in Kansas and Merritt was talking of going there.

Kansas was in conflict. Would it be a slave state or a free one? The antislavery forces in New England were so worried over the danger of tipping the political balance towards the extension of slavery that they were paying the travel and homestead money for antislavery settlers such as the young Anthony sons to move to Kansas.

Mary was spending all her free time from teaching in helping the abolitionist movement; she also volunteered to do what she could to help Susan.

As soon as the harvest was over Susan's father went with her to Seneca Falls. Daniel Anthony enjoyed the company of Henry Stanton as much as Susan did that of Mrs. Stanton. They were a congenial group as the two women worked over the speeches Susan would have to make on her petition campaign. While Mrs. Stanton worked at her desk Susan frequently took charge of the children.

But if Susan deferred to her friend for the writing of speeches and pamphlets, Elizabeth Cady Stanton was astounded at the plans for the campaign which Susan all alone was making. No one had done anything like this before. No one had ever shown herself to be the executive that Susan B. Anthony was.

Calmly she planned a succession of meetings and talks in town after town throughout New York. Notices were sent out to the newspapers in each town; halls or church rooms or civic meeting places were hired.

When everything was arranged a meeting was called in Rochester and the petition was submitted to the women attending for their approval and signatures. Susan promised them that when she had collected several thousand signatures the petition would be submitted to the state legislature.

The November gathering unanimously approved the petition, and Wendell Phillips gave a small amount of money. The rest of Susan's expenses—the hall rentals and newspaper advertisements—were paid for by her father, but she was determined to take only a little from him and make her own way as she went along. She would travel by train, by stagecoach and sometimes by wagon or sleigh or horseback. If a sympathizer lived in a town where she would speak, she might be able to stay in a home; otherwise, she had to use public taverns and inns.

Her first experience was typical of many that followed. It was in a small town in Chatauqua County, western New York. The weather was miserable. Audiences for both the afternoon and the evening meetings were disappointingly small. What was worse, she had to spend fifty-six cents for four pounds of candles to light the room in the courthouse, since the custodian informed her that her rent did not cover candles or oil lamps.

What she collected in admission money did not cover expenses. Yet she got signatures on one petition and was able to leave two more of the petition forms with a husband and wife who had never come to a woman's rights meeting before, but assured her they would help by getting signatures from their friends and would then mail them to Mrs. Stanton.

On she went. At her next stop, in the town of Sherman, the weather was milder and more people came to see and hear her. She knew that most came out of curiosity. A woman traveling alone, a woman speaker, a woman talking about changing laws—it was as good as a freak show or circus, they thought. Susan did not care, so long as they came. Among the audiences were always a few thoughtful people and even some brave enough to agree with her.

In one way Susan did not live up to expectations. Both she and Mrs. Stanton had given up wearing the bloomer costume, and Susan had, thankfully, gone back to her modest but attractive dresses. She missed the freedom of the trousers, but she did not miss the mockery and the jeering.

She had booked meetings every other night; sometimes every night, which meant snatching sleep wherever and whenever she could, frequently while sitting up in a railroad car or a stagecoach. In some towns the postmaster and the sheriff were very cooperative, and Susan would arrive to see her handbills and notices already pasted up in the courthouse and post office bulletin boards and other public places. The newspapers would already be carrying her paid advertisements and perhaps a free story about her. As a result, there would be a good crowd; sometimes a good collection of money.

A resort town such as Saratoga Springs paid well, especially in late spring when the race track was about to open. Wealthy people flocked there to drink the mineral waters, parade their fashionable clothes and get ready for the horse racing season. Still—in an age when there was no television or radio or many other forms of amusement—the rich were bored. It was an evening's amusement to attend one of those meetings of Miss Anthony's, and they paid well for the privilege.

Even among these people Susan found some who really listened to what she said and cared enough to sign her petition. She felt as if each visit to each town was like throwing a pebble into a pool. Long after she left the circles widened and widened—the words spread and ideas began to change.

The newspaper in one town, the *Roundout Courier,* described one of her larger meetings:

At the appointed hour a lady, unattended and unheralded, quietly glided in and ascended the platform. She was as easy and self-possessed as a lady should always be when performing a plain duty, even under 600 curious eyes. The custodian had dumped some tracts and papers on the platform. Miss Anthony gathered them up composedly, placed them on a table, put her decorous shawl on one chair and a bonnet on another, sat a moment, smoothed her hair discreetly, and then deliberately walked to the table and addressed the audience. She wore a becoming black silk dress, gracefully draped and made with a basque waist. She is of pleasing, rather than pretty, features, decidedly expressive countenance, rich brown hair very effectively and not elaborately arranged; her voice modulated and musical, her style earnest and impressive.

Susan had also decided to let her hair grow. Worn in a roll at the back of her head it was more becoming, and almost as easy to fix, as when short.

Susan read this description of herself and was pleased that none of her actual anxiety ever showed. When the editor wrote that she "sat a moment, smoothed her hair discreetly, and then deliberately walked to the table," evidently no one in the audience guessed at the courage it took for her to walk to that table and address them.

SUSAN B. ANTHONY

She still considered herself a poor public speaker. She could remember and talk about facts and figures and true stories of real hardships, but it seemed to her that she lacked any emotional oratorical style. She used plain, blunt language.

The courage to speak would have been difficult enough for Susan, but no audience or newspaper reporter had any idea of what she had gone through to reach the town and to appear "composed" and "decorous," with her clothes presentable and herself clean and tidy.

Traveling conditions in the dead of winter were incredibly arduous. Most towns were not on the railroad and could only be reached by sleigh or coach. In spite of lap robes and a heavy coat and boots, Susan was always chilled. She beat her hands together. She thumped her sides and her knees and her legs in order to keep the circulation going and to prevent chilblains and actual freezing.

Sometimes she welcomed the moments when the snowdrifts were so deep the horse could not make headway through them. Then, while the driver and the male passengers went ahead and shoveled a path for horse and vehicle, she could walk behind. If she was the only passenger she could grab a shovel and work with the driver. He might be shocked, but he was grateful, and she could get warm for a few moments.

After such long, bitter, miserable rides she would come to the town inn or hotel. If the innkeeper and his wife disapproved of her as a bold and forward hussy, she would be given a bedroom without a fire and would have to huddle inside the bedcovers for hours before she could get warm enough to sleep.

If she was in a stagecoach carrying regular passengers and

making regular stops at taverns and inns during the day, she noticed the men got out and were welcomed in the warm rooms, but their wives had to stay outside! It was not considered proper for them to go into a tavern. They stayed outside and ate the cold food they had brought along or waited patiently until their menfolks brought them some bread and cheese.

But not Miss Susan B. Anthony! She got out when the men did; she went into the warm building; she demanded that the tavernkeeper bring her the same hot food he served the men.

"Have you no shame, woman?" one innkeeper shouted at her.

"None," she replied. "But I do have a good appetite."

It was at night, when she stopped to sleep in these wayside inns, that she was made to feel the full indignity of the treatment given to a woman traveling alone.

She would be given the worst room in the house, with no fireplace or chimney to heat it. If she asked for a hot brick wrapped in flannel, the chambermaid would "forget" to bring it and Susan had to crawl in between unwarmed, icy sheets. In the mornings the room would be so cold the water in the pitcher would be frozen. She would have to break the ice on top in order to pour the rest of the water into the basin. Never, not even under the worst circumstances, did she neglect her morning sponge bath. This was not just for cleanliness. It was for her morale. She felt if she once let down her standards, she would just give in and go home.

While she traveled she observed. The treatment given her she could endure. She was traveling of her own accord. But she saw how the world treated women, and she used these examples when she spoke.

"At one inn where I stopped for the night," she told her audiences, "the woman of the house did all the work for the travelers, cooking for them and serving and washing up, making beds and cleaning rooms, while at the same time she took care of her own small children. Her husband did nothing. He sat and smoked and chatted with the male travelers. Yet when the time came to pay, when I offered the money to the wife, the husband came and snatched it. He was quite indignant that I should offer it to her, not to him."

If Susan had to endure harsh treatment from many individuals, she also found unexpected kindnesses. In Albany, where she spoke to a large gathering, a wealthy and cultured Quaker gentleman was in the audience, and he came forward to sign her petition. When she took the stage the next morning to Lake George for her meeting the next day, she found the same Quaker was her fellow-passenger and that he had had a thick plank of wood heated through to place under her feet.

Oh, how good it felt! She wondered how he had come to think of such a good idea, and how he had known she would be on that stage. The warmth of the plank seeped right through the soles of her boots and her toes stayed warm. At each rest stop or luncheon stop her new friend took the plank inside and insisted the tavernkeeper reheat it for Susan.

She began to suspect he was not on that stage by accident, because all day long he asked questions of her: about her family, her teaching career, her attitudes towards keeping house, as well as her ideas and her present campaign. The more they talked, the more he admired her.

She said good-bye to him when she reached her destina-

72

tion, and hurried about getting everything ready for her afternoon and evening meeting. At the close of the meeting who should appear but her new friend—and with a fine sleigh heaped with fur robes and drawn by two beautiful grey horses. She was to be his houseguest that night; he would not take no for an answer. He drove her to his beautiful home and introduced her to his sister, who kept house for him.

The next day was Sunday. Susan was persuaded to stay and let him drive her on Monday to her next meeting in a nearby town. Susan accepted gladly. It was wonderful to be with such kindly people, in a home of great comfort and culture.

On the drive on Monday he asked her to marry him. She would be his beloved wife, protected and sheltered. He admired and shared her ideas; he would have no objection to their attending antislavery meetings and woman's rights meetings, together. The only thing was, of course, that she had to discontinue this madness of her winter lecture tour.

No cause, he told her, was worth the cold, the misery and the humiliations she was enduring. It was too great a strain on a female's physical and emotional strength.

Susan knew well that she was suffering physically. Emotionally?—never. She was doing what she had to do and doing it well; there was even a pride that she was doing something no one else could or would. She was not even tempted to accept his proposal.

Gently and tactfully she told him no, thanking him with all her heart for his offer. After she left him, having had that taste of comfort and kindness, she felt even more keenly the hardships of the next weeks. The weather worsened. She rode through blizzards. The cold wind and snow drifted into the stagecoach, and she shook until she grew too numb to feel anything.

At one stop she could not be sure that her feet were not frozen. She persuaded the tavern woman to let her take off her boots in the kitchen and let cold water run over her legs and feet. There was no feeling. In a panic, Susan took sticks from the wood box and beat her toes, ankles and legs until at last she could feel some sensation in them.

The returning circulation caused acute pain, but the woman of the tavern had warmed flannel and now she wrapped Susan's feet in them. Since this mad Miss Anthony insisted that she had to go on when the stage was ready, they left the warm flannel on and pulled the boots over them. Hobbling, Susan managed to get back to the stage, crawl in and make it to the next town and her meeting.

After that day her feet were in such bad shape that she had to give them this soaking, beating, heating treatment every night before she went to bed. In the mornings her legs ached; gradually her whole back pained her so badly she could hardly stand upright.

On the way to the town of Malone she had to lean forward and hang onto the seat in front in order to relieve the agony in her back; if she relaxed or sat back in the sleigh, her spine was so jolted the pain was intolerable.

Yet she went on and managed her meetings and gathered names on her petitions, until at Ogdensburg she simply could not get out of bed by herself. Luckily she was staying there with cousins. Since she was determined to keep her next engagement at Canton, her cousin's wife and sister-in-law had to ease her out of bed, dress her and comb her hair.

Her cousin carried her out to the sleigh. She was then

driven seventeen miles to Canton, sitting doubled up with her head on her knees. Yet, so great was her will and her sense of duty, that she stood and conducted her meeting as usual that day.

If people wondered why Miss Anthony stood rigid and held onto the back of a chair, it was only a passing wonder in their thoughts. They had no idea that it was the only way she *could* stand; she could not have moved without crying out.

Susan had heard of the "water cure." A relative of hers treated patients in this way. She decided to try it.

At a hotel in Watertown she ordered the chambermaid to bring up a tub and buckets of ice water to her room, then sent her down again for hot blankets. Susan inched her way out of bed and into the tub. When the maid returned she found the woman sitting in the ice-cold water. "Pour it over my back," ordered Susan. The horrified maid did as she was told, then helped to wrap the hot, hot blankets about Susan's wet body and roll her into bed.

It worked. Susan had her first good night's sleep in weeks, and woke feeling somewhat better. Her legs still hurt and her back gave her trouble, but on she went, fulfilling every engagement, going from town to town.

By the first of May she came home triumphant. She had lectured and circulated petitions in 54 of the state's 60 counties; had collected thousands and thousands of signatures; had taken in $2,367 in admissions and spent $2,291; and had a balance of $76. She had a right to feel triumphant.

Susan B. Anthony had done something no woman had ever done before and had done it very much on her own, but she had left behind her not only new workers for woman's rights and new local groups, but enormous interest.

SUSAN B. ANTHONY

Not only were such people as Lucy Stone and Elizabeth Cady Stanton amazed and proud of their protégé; the leaders of the antislavery organization woke up to the fact that Daniel Anthony's daughter could do more than bake the best peach cobbler. She had talents they wanted. She was an organizer and a doer.

Even such noted speakers as Abby and Stephen Foster had made only five or six speeches on a lecture tour. Susan had made hundreds.

Chapter Five

In the early part of the summer the Anthonys tried to get Susan to rest. She was still bothered with rheumatic pains, but they all thought the summer heat and the easy work would help. At first it did, but then the overstrain of the winter caught up with her again. As soon as she tried to help around the farm her legs and back felt crippled.

Her cousin, Seth Rogers, ran a Hydropathic Institute in Worcester, Massachusetts; it was through him she had heard of the "water cure." Now she went to Worcester and put herself completely in his hands. The last winter's campaign had done so well she was determined to start another in the last months of 1855 and the early ones of 1856.

She was as disciplined in healing herself as she had been in campaigning, and she stuck to her cousin's health regime. Whether it was the ice water and the relaxing heat of the blankets, or whether it was that for the first time in her life she was ordered to rest in bed, and did so, all or part of this healed her completely.

During those weeks Susan had a marvelously lazy time. She read. She slept. When she began to feel better her cousin took her on long carriage rides through the beautiful

October foliage. By November she was fit and ready for her second petition campaign.

She had already arranged to do this when she was asked by the American Antislavery Society to drop everything else and work for them, instead. She was sorely tempted to do so. Slavery was such a crucial issue! She wrote the Reverend Samuel J. May that she would, if she could get other woman's rights speakers to make the winter campaign.

Lucy Stone had promised; so had Antoinette Brown. Suddenly, both women married, and Lucy moved to Ohio. Both were much too busy with their new husbands and new lives to go on any speaking tour. Susan B. Anthony had to fill all the engagements herself, even when half-mad with a new anxiety.

She and her whole family were terribly worried about Merritt. He had gone to Kansas and there he had met the great John Brown and become one of his adherents. That meant Merritt was in the midst of the boiling cauldron. In Kansas people didn't talk pro-slavery or antislavery; they met in physical skirmishes.

As the West opened up and new states were created, the issue of free states or slave states became vital. There was a bill now before Congress to make Kansas and Nebraska slave states. Agitation for or against, in Mississippi or Alabama or in the New England states, could have some effect on the congressional decision, but the sentiment inside Kansas and Nebraska was what would tip the scales.

So Susan and the rest of the Anthonys waited for letters from Merritt and watched the newspapers. In May the pro-slavery men attacked the town of Lawrence, burning a hotel, breaking up newspaper offices and printing presses and pillaging the homes of antislavery people. In retaliation,

John Brown and his men, four of whom were his own sons, attacked pro-slavery colonists at Pottawatomie Creek. Rochester and New York papers carried the story, but without any mention of Merritt Anthony.

Then three hundred pro-slavers attacked John Brown's colony at Osawatomie Creek, and Susan knew Merritt had to be involved. His homestead was right there, at the very spot.

No word came. It was an agonizing time. There were estimates of two hundred killed in the free state settlement.

Finally a letter arrived from Merritt. He had, indeed, been in the fight in spite of having been seriously ill at the time. He had fought until he could fight no longer and his strength gave out and he lay unconscious. He came to, dragged himself under some shelter and then fainted again. When he recovered, the fight was over. On hands and knees he crawled to his cabin. There he had lain ill and alone and unattended for weeks, until he had recovered.

Susan wrote him: "Words cannot tell how often we think of you or how sadly we feel that the terrible crime of this nation against humanity is being avenged on the heads of our sons and brothers. . . ."

There were some antislavery forces who condemned John Brown's tactics, but Susan was not one of them. Like Frederick Douglass and Garrison and Wendell Phillips she felt there could be no compromise. There had to be a complete end to slavery now, at whatever cost.

Susan found that her woman's rights meetings were poorly attended, and she understood why. She herself, while she grimly continued the task of getting signatures, was thinking of the coming election and what it would mean to the country. The young Republican Party had put forth Colonel

John C. Fremont as their candidate on an antislavery platform. He lost by 500,000 votes.

In November James Buchanan was elected president of the United States, and the slaveholders were jubilant. In December Susan B. Anthony wrote the Reverend May that she would give up her other work; she was ready to become an organizer for the Antislavery Committee.

"I shall be very glad," she wrote, "if I am able to render even the most humble service to this cause. Heaven knows there is need of earnest, effective, radical workers."

The Reverend May replied immediately: "We put all New York into your control and want your name on all letters and your hand in all arrangements." She was given very capable speakers, such as Parker Pillsbury, Stephen Foster, Abby Kelley Foster and two Blacks: Charles Remond and his sister, Sarah Remond, and was told to plan their meetings and make the schedules for their tours.

Her group were all dedicated men and women, but they simply could not stand the pace she set for them. They tried their best. It just seemed unreasonable to them that they should speak in one town one night, drive from midnight until dawn to the next place, get a couple of hours sleep at best and then face a hostile, arguing crowd that evening. They complained to the Committee. They were only human. They missed their appointments.

Parker Pillsbury quit entirely, then—shamed by Susan's own example—came back to finish his tour.

She well knew that her speakers had reason to complain. She was on an arranged tour as tightly scheduled as was theirs and she knew what they were going through. In addition to the hardships of winter travel, they all faced angry, bullying crowds.

SUSAN B. ANTHONY

On the question of slavery none were neutral. They were either aggressively against or defiantly for; both sides came to the meetings, which often ended in a shouting match across the room.

Her own speech would get lost in the turmoil; she would stand on the platform, helpless, and listen and watch while the meeting degenerated into a furious debate in which no side listened to the other, but all tried to outshout each other. Names were called. As the speaker and organizer, Susan came in for more than her share of such abuse.

If the antislavery people outnumbered the pro-slavers then there might be a chance to be heard, and Susan could leave with some feeling of having done well. But if her audience was mainly hostile to her, she was in for trouble. Insults were the very least she could expect.

Once a gang of men raided her meeting hall, with sticks and clubs in their hands, and drove her small, friendly audience out. The gang then started to "give her a lesson," but she stood so quietly, with such dignity, just looking at them, that they only muttered to themselves and went away. She had won something of a moral victory over them, but her meeting was ruined.

Another time pepper was thrown on a hot stove. The audience sneezed and coughed, and the bullies jeered at them from the windows. In another town she found her meeting hall door padlocked. When she went to get a key the hostile men surrounded her and threatened to ride her out of town on a rail. Antislavery people had to break through the circle, rescue her and stand guard while she opened the hall and went to her place to speak.

One day she arrived in a town to find all her posters torn down and her handbills destroyed. She got in touch with local Quakers and they assured her there would be a good crowd at her meeting; they would pass the word to all their neighbors. But when the door was opened, and before Susan and her kind friends could enter, a gang of men rushed in, went to the platform, dragged up chairs around the desk she would have used and began to play cards, shouting and laughing and smoking cigars. The police had to be called to evict them and allow her meeting to go on.

Some sheriffs and town constables were helpful; others just stood by and allowed ruffians to close her halls or disrupt her speeches. Some newspapers were openly on her side and printed notices of her meetings and editorial comments; opposing newspapers warned everyone to stay away from that "crazy woman" who ought to be home where she belonged. Who was paying her to stir up all this agitation, they wanted to know.

She was being paid $10 a month by the Antislavery Committee. Although she took up collections wherever she went (and she knew herself to be a good money-raiser), the collections did not meet the expenses of newspaper notices, handbills, posters and hall rentals.

The one good dress she wore was a ten-year-old merino which she had bought in Canajoharie, and which she now dyed a dark green. She had to ask her father to help her out in paying for her transportation and hotel bills. Daniel Anthony was more than willing, and she should not have felt guilty about asking, since she worked every summer on the farm. Yet her pride was hurt in having to ask for help.

"Every woman should have a purse of her own," she often said, and had used as a slogan for her petition campaign. It was not fine clothes she wanted; she did not resent being paid so little by the Antislavery Society, since its funds were so limited; she only craved independence.

The 1857 campaign trip ended with a deficit of a thousand dollars for the Antislavery Society, but the executive committee felt Susan's job had been well worth every penny they had to raise to meet the debt. The secretary of the Society wrote to her in the spring, when she was back in Rochester: "We have made the following a committee of arrangements for the annual meeting: Garrison, Phillips, Edmund Quincy, Johnson and Susan B. Anthony."

Susan stared at that letter. She had felt tired and discouraged. Now she was seized by a feeling this could not be true; this could not be happening to her; that she, Susan B. Anthony, who used to make the peach pies and serve the table for her father's distinguished guests, should be placed on the roster beside these people. She was one of the leaders!

To be on the national committee with such famous people! Could she have really deserved such an honor?

Susan was not overly modest. She knew she could organize meetings, raise money and leave behind her a group inspired to do more than they had before, but she still thought of herself as a poor speaker, and no leader. Actually she was growing quick-witted and quick-tongued.

At one meeting a Quaker from Virginia rose to admonish her for her fiery agitation. He defended slavery. He criticized Susan for her ruthless abolitionist stand. "Christ was no agitator, but a peacemaker," he told her sternly.

Susan flared back at him: "Read the New Testament and say if Christ was not an agitator! 'I came into this world not to bring peace but a sword . . . Who is this among us crying 'Peace, peace when there is no peace'? Woe unto you, scribes and Pharisees, hypocrites . . . !' "

Daniel Anthony's daughter knew her Bible well.

Another time she grew tired of the same old, old question put to her so many times: "What will the country do with all those black savages if they are immediately emancipated?"

She flung the question right back at her tormentor. "But if you emancipate the slaves, what will you do with them? What will the black man do with himself is the question for *him* to answer. I am yet to learn that the Saxon man is the great reservoir of human rights, to be doled out at his discretion to the nations of the earth. Do with the Negroes? What arrogance in us to put the question! What shall we do with a race of men and women who have fed, clothed and supported both themselves and their oppressors for centuries!" It was a powerful answer, to which there was no rebuttal.

In March, 1857 came the Dred Scott decision of the Supreme Court, which denied that any Negro, free or not, could be considered a citizen with a citizen's rights, nor could a black man become free by living in a free state. In fact, no state was any longer "free." The slave was a man's property no matter if it was Georgia or Massachusetts—or any territory about to become a state.

This was a serious blow to the abolition movement. The government was declaring itself on the side of the slave states.

The Antislavery Society knew they had to make an all-out effort to combat the trend. Again they asked Susan to make another winter campaign and plan lecture tours for other speakers. She agreed.

In spite of all the hardships, she felt that winter's campaign had been a great success. Many new people were outraged at the Supreme Court's decision and the government's concessions to slavery. In the trail of all her speakers new local antislavery groups sprang up.

But oh! how good it was when it was over and she could

go back to the farm, take off her lecture clothes, put on her kitchen dress and cook herself some really good food!

She wrote to Lucy Stone in Ohio (who had shocked America by keeping her own name when she married Henry Blackwell): "Here I am once more in my own Farm Home, where my weary head rests upon my own home pillows. . . . I had been gone Four Months, scarcely sleeping the second night under the same roof."

Susan worked in her raspberry and strawberry beds and in the vegetable garden, and wandered with her father out to the orchard to see the flowering of the peach, cherry, plum, apple and pear trees and to estimate their crop. She cooked and cleaned and was once more the happy daughter of a close family, loved and appreciated and admired. Susan Anthony needed this to prepare her for what was to come.

As a Quaker she was opposed to war and bloodshed, but as an Abolitionist she anticipated the stern necessity of war as the only means of emancipating the slaves, since the slave-owners' attitude would not yield to words or reason. Out in Illinois a tall, homely lawyer had suddenly become a name in Eastern newspapers because of his debates with Stephen A. Douglas. "A house divided against itself cannot stand. I believe this government cannot endure permanently half slave and half free," said Abraham Lincoln.

The Republican Party hailed him, but Susan was wary of any politician. They were too apt, she thought, to make compromises for political tricks. Even James Buchanan had said slavery was morally wrong! Yet he yielded to the slave states on every issue.

Susan had little patience with anyone who put his personal ambition or his personal life ahead of the burning moral issues of the day. She was even provoked and critical of Lucy Stone Blackwell and Antoinette Brown for beginning their families of babies. Since Mrs. Stanton had by now produced her fifth child, too, Susan was annoyed with all of them. If all the woman's rights leaders were going to be tied down by caring for babies, who was there but Susan to carry on the work? Along with all her back-breaking labors for the Antislavery Society, she had to plan the 1858 Woman's Rights convention in New York almost single-handed—in addition to helping organize the Antislavery convention which would precede it.

She wasn't quite so annoyed with Elizabeth Cady Stanton as with the others, since Mrs. Stanton continued to do what she could and was always ready with sound advice. When Susan had been asked by the New York Teachers Association to make a speech at their annual meeting, the two women rightly considered this a major triumph since it was a turnabout from the year when the Association's president had been outraged that she had dared to rise to ask a question.

Susan rushed to Seneca Falls when she got the invitation, and Mrs. Stanton settled at her desk with pen and paper to plan Susan's speech. It was a highly controversial one, and the newspapers were full of it after Susan's appearance.

She had advocated coeducational schools; financial support for girl students as well as for boys; higher education for women. Then she had demanded that black teachers, women or men, should not be discriminated against but should be allowed to teach in any school, white or black.

Mr. Henry Stanton read the report in his morning newspaper and remarked to his wife: "Well, my dear, another notice of Susan. You stir up Susan and she stirs up the world."

The two 1858 conventions held in New York—the Anti-slavery Society and the Woman's Rights conventions, were very successful, in spite of the attempts of mobs to invade the hall. Since most of the leadership of the Antislavery Society was also friendly to the cause of woman suffrage, Susan easily roped in such famous speakers as Wendell Phillips, Thomas Wentworth Higginson and George William Curtis along with Lucretia Mott and Ernestine Rose. But much of the success of the conventions was due to Susan's planning and calmness as chairman when hecklers tried to interrupt the meeting.

She impressed one man very greatly.

In December, Wendell Phillips wrote her the astounding news that a donor, who wished to remain anonymous, had given him $5000 for the woman's rights cause. Phillips, Susan B. Anthony and Lucy Stone had been named by the giver of the money as the committee to decide how it was to be spent. Susan went around for a while in a daze of happiness. It was a great thrill to announce the gift to all the other women who had worked for the cause.

Unfortunately, spreading the word about it also spread some problems. Every woman had her own pet theory of where the money could be best spent: some wanted it to endow scholarships for girls to attend academies; some wanted it to be a legal fund to help women in need of lawyers; others wanted it for the publishing of books about the struggle of women to be free and equal.

They were all good causes. They all needed money. But Susan insisted that the first draft upon the money, in the amount of $1500, should be spent to further the drive to get more signatures to more petitions for women's rights to their own property, their own wages and to the guardianship of their children. Word had come to Mrs. Stanton that some of the New York legislators were changing their minds and favoring the petition. Another big push might see the laws changed. Some state senators promised their help.

Wendell Phillips backed Susan against all the pleas and demands of other women leaders. He could do this because he alone knew that the donor—Francis Jackson—was in favor of anything Miss Anthony wanted done.

All through the year of 1859 Susan was busy getting signatures, rolling up thousands and thousands of new names and new supporters.

This was a year of new hope for women, but it was also a year of tragedy, in the other cause so close to Susan's heart, and to a man she passionately admired.

In October came the news of John Brown's raid on Harper's Ferry, the killing of his two sons and the arrest of the old, white-bearded, giant-hearted man, along with the brave Shields Green, an escaped slave.

Merritt was not with Brown; he had stayed on to work in Kansas. To the Anthony family, however, the fate of John Brown and his men was a personal matter. They knew him. Because of their close association with Frederick Douglass, they may have known beforehand of John Brown's plan. The raid on Harper's Ferry was to have been the signal for slaves to run away from their matsers and join John Brown in mountain fortresses where they could maintain themselves in freedom.

The raid, the killings and the arrest, the trial and the sentence of death upon Brown, hit America like a shock wave. Wild rumors were spread: that the raid was to start a slave revolt, an uprising to murder slave owners; that it was a giant conspiracy. Letters of Frederick Douglass were found in Brown's possession and Douglass had to flee the country to avoid being tried for conspiracy.

In Rochester the Anthonys and their circle of friends also came under suspicion. This did not frighten Susan. She planned a public memorial meeting if the sentence of death was carried out. She went from house to house to announce her meeting; although she went only to people who were known to be antislavery, many of them slammed the door in her face, in fear. Susan went steadfastly on.

John Brown was hanged on Friday, December 2, 1859, and that night the Rochester memorial meeting was held. Since she had had difficulty getting well-known speakers to come, Susan presided. The small, courageous group pledged itself to continue the struggle for John Brown's ideal of freedom.

Certainly Susan B. Anthony kept that pledge. There was nothing the Antislavery Society asked of her that she would not do, if she had time. At this moment, though, she had to concentrate on the woman's rights petitions.

Ansen Bingham, chairman of the judiciary committee of the New York state legislature, wrote Mrs. Stanton, informing her that he intended to bring in a report favorable to the bills fashioned out of the petition wording. He urged Mrs. Stanton to be ready to present her strongest arguments to the legislature before it voted. He would see that she had the chance to speak.

Susan promptly moved to Seneca Falls and into the Stanton home. Again the two women faced each other across the desk and went to work.

Mrs. Stanton had the magic in her voice to move an audience emotionally, but legislators would vote on facts, and it

SUSAN B. ANTHONY

was the facts Susan dug up. She went to newspaper offices
and libraries; she wrote to factories and mills to get statistics
on working women.

It was a popular myth of the day that women did *not* work,
except in the home or teaching school; therefore, there was
no need of laws to protect their wages or salaries. Susan had
to prove that this was a myth.

Up and down streets she went, making sample surveys,
popping in and out of shops and stores. The husband's name
was on the shop, but in a great many places the wife and
daughters did the work. The money, of course, went to the
man. Susan had already gathered a great deal of such factual
cases during her travels. These facts went into the notes from
which Mrs. Stanton was frantically trying to put together a
speech.

Susan went to lawyers and judges. "What happens," she
asked them, "if a woman must leave her husband because
of his brutality or unfaithfulness?"

"He can force her to come back to him. He can keep the
children from her. If she leaves and opens a shop or earns
wages, he can come and take the money from her." These
were the answers. They supplied her with case histories to
prove her points.

A New York state Woman's Rights Convention was held
February 3rd and 4th of 1860 in Albany, the state capital.
From the resolute women who gathered there, various ones
were assigned to talk to every member of the judiciary committee and every other legislator who would listen to them.
Ansen Bingham came through with his promise: Mrs. Stanton
was invited to address a joint session of the Senate and Assembly.

On March 19, dressed in her best suit and hat, looking tiny

and winsome, her hair curled and her cheeks dimpling, Elizabeth Cady Stanton walked up to the front of the legislative chamber, put her notes on the speaker's lectern and said: "Gentlemen, I have a petition to present to you for redress of grievances . . ."

And she launched into her speech.

The legislators sat stunned. That such a petite, dimpling lady could hurl such fierce words at them was amazing, but how could she—or any woman—know so much, use such logic and possess such facts? She gave them instance after instance of fathers who took the earnings of their daughters who worked in factories; of widows turned out of their houses by their sons; of husbands who overworked and abused their wives, made them earn money and took it from them; of wives powerless to protect their children from a father's abuse because they had no guardianship and he did.

So marvelous was her speech that the legislature broke out into involuntary applause when she finished.

Within a very few days the exhausted Susan and Mrs. Stanton heard the great news: a bill had passed both the Senate and Assembly which gave them even more than they had asked for!

Under the new law a married woman had the right to hold property, real and personal, without the husband claiming it or interfering with her handling of it. A wife could work for wages or carry on a trade or profession and keep her own earnings. Married women could enter into contracts under their own names; they could buy or sell without permission. If there was sufficient cause of habitual drunkenness, cruelty, insanity or criminality, a woman could separate from her husband and run her own affairs and keep her own money. A wife was joint guardian with her husband of their children.

If a husband died, the wife had the same rights over children and property that her husband would have had if she had died first.

It was victory. But Susan, back on the lecture circuit for the antislavery cause, had no time to celebrate.

Chapter Six

In November, 1860 Abraham Lincoln was elected President of the United States. In that same month South Carolina voted to secede. By January, 1861 other Southern states had followed suit, and on February 9 Jefferson Davis was elected president of the Confederacy. Fort Sumter was fired upon. The war had begun.

All during the winter before Lincoln was inaugurated, Susan and the Reverend Samuel J. May, Stephen Foster and Elizabeth Cady Stanton held meetings. Other leaders edited newspapers or held big-city meetings or worked prominently in the new Republican Party, but these four covered the small towns and villages of New York and New England.

This year Susan could feel that the majority of Northerners were coming to accept war if it meant that war was the only way of keeping the Southern states in the Union, but those who hated the Abolitionists for "stirring up all this trouble" hated them more venomously than ever.

At Susan's third speaking date news of her arrival had preceded her. She stepped out of the stagecoach to see a stuffed dummy hanging by the neck from a lamppost. It was labeled "Susan B. Anthony," and it was a cruel caricature of an ugly woman, almost witchlike. As she walked to her hotel something struck her on the back.

From its sulfuric smell she knew it was a rotten egg. She took off her coat and wiped it with her handkerchief, but she never stopped walking, never broke her stride, showing nothing in her face. She passed two men at the hotel entrance. One spat at her, the other said: "Silly old bitch!" She pretended not to notice or hear.

But once up in her hotel room she sat on her bed until her body stopped trembling. Then she took off her hat and looked at herself in the cracked mirror over the washstand. Was she really so ugly? So witchlike?

At forty she had no vanity but she did have pride. She studied her face with a critical eye. Pretty? No, she had never been that. But the years had not hardened her. Her skin was smooth. Being schooled to a serene countenance there were not many laugh lines around her mouth, but neither were there lines of ill-temper or discontent.

Her deepset eyes still looked out steadily from under the straight line of her eyebrows; she wore her hair in the neat way of old: parted in the center and pulled back. A little grey made thin streaks at the sides.

The slim suppleness of youth was gone, but she had scarcely put on an ounce of weight. Now she had the thin, muscular firmness of tough whipcord and the unyielding straightness of her spine. Hidden by a decent, suitable dress and softened at collar and cuffs, her thinness gave her distinction, even if she had no grace.

"You're no picture postcard," said Susan to her image in the mirror, "but you're not something to scare the crows with, either." She turned away, satisfied with her own self-respect. She was even able to force herself that night to introduce herself at the meeting with humor, as the real Susan B. Anthony, not the stuffed dummy her audience had seen hanging from the lamppost.

It was not always easy to find something humorous in the attacks against her when she was struck with clods of earth outside her meeting halls or when men yelled obscene words at her, when she was hissed and booed so loudly she could not go on with her speeches. In some towns the police escorted her to the train for her own safety.

Susan was not the only one to suffer, of course. Frederick Douglass had returned from abroad to take up his work. His *North Star* newspaper windows were broken, and he was constantly in physical danger when he campaigned for Lincoln. Wendell Phillips was pursued by mobs. William Lloyd Garrison was frequently ill, under the strain of so many years of antislavery agitation and violent abuse.

He did not even have the satisfaction that Douglass had in the emerging Republican Party. Garrison had no faith in any political party, and Susan agreed with him absolutely. She spoke with tartness over Lincoln's slow approach to emancipation.

Once the actual war began there was a temporary lull in speech-making. Action was the keyword, as men rushed into local regiments and were sent off to Washington, sure of a quick and easy victory. With so many men off the farms, and labor hard to get, Susan's place was on the farm in Rochester.

Daniel Anthony made a trip out to Kansas and returned with the news that Daniel, Jr., was a Lieutenant-Colonel in the Union Army, and Merritt was a captain in the 7th Cavalry of Kansas. Both were on active duty.

Susan threw herself into the farm and housework, feeling this was the best sacrifice she could make at the moment. She planted and hoed and weeded; she cooked and scrubbed and sewed. She wove yards of rag carpet. When she could find nothing else upon which to spend her energy she mended and varnished old furniture. Along with the other women of Rochester she spent hours rolling bandages and making up kits of useful objects for the soldiers at the battlefront.

Both Daniel and Lucy Anthony left her alone to work out her frustrations in physical labor. They were glad of her help, since her mother was not always well, but they could sympathize that she was unhappy that life was once more passing her by, and her talents were being wasted in blacking the kitchen stove and painting the kitchen steps.

To add to her personal discouragement, the war was not the quick, easy victory as expected. Then, as if she weren't unhappy enough, an angry letter came from Mrs. Stanton, with bad news from another quarter.

In April, 1862, new legislators in Albany took advantage of the fact that people were thinking only of war and not of other matters, and they amended the act of 1860, repealing that section of it which had given mothers equal guardianship of their children, and widows control over the property of minor children. Susan and Mrs. Stanton saw the fruits of their victory nibbled away.

The war was going badly for the North, and it had settled down into a grim struggle. Men died and some families became bitter. Why should white men die because of black slaves? At the same time the Abolitionist newspapers pleaded and railed at Lincoln and the Congress because they did not proclaim the slaves free and allow the freed slaves to enlist and fight for their own freedom.

Black men wanted to fight but, so far, whether they were legally free or runaways, they had been used by the army only as labor forces, without uniform or respect.

Then, suddenly, there came whispers and talk of emancipation. Word traveled swiftly to all antislavery workers in every Northern town: it was coming! And on September 18, 1862, Daniel Anthony came home early, driving his carriage up to the farm door and calling: "Susan, come quickly! Susan . . . !"

She and her mother hurried to him, one from the kitchen, the other from her sitting room. Their faces were pale. Every day they feared to hear that something dreadful had befallen Merritt or his older brother. But they were relieved by the broad smile on Daniel Anthony's face. He waved a newspaper.

"It is Emancipation! It has come at last. The president has announced his intention that slavery be abolished by federal law. He has done the courageous thing, because the Southern rebels now know they cannot surrender and still keep their slaves. The war will be fought until surrender is unconditional," he said.

"Now," Susan exulted, "there can be Negro soldiers and Negro regiments!"

And there were. Regiments of all black soldiers and regiments of mixed black and white were formed. No one fought more bravely than the man who was fighting for his own freedom.

The Proclamation, however, was only a notice of intention by the president. It would take a congressional vote of both the Senate and House before it could become law in the form of an amendment to the Constitution. Many in Congress either did not approve of emancipation or else thought this was not the time for it.

Pro-slavery elements in Congress would fight against it. "So will those," Susan told her parents and Mary, "who want to reconcile the South and bring her back into the Union, at no matter what cost. They will start yelling: 'bring the South back! let them keep slavery!' "

"And thee," said her father, as he glanced at what she was sewing under the oil lamp, "are preparing thy old gowns to go forth and answer them. Are thee not, Susan?"

"I must. Mrs. Stanton agrees with me: we must put Northern women to work." It was a November night and snowing outside. The family was grouped around the fireplace. The knitting needles of both Mrs. Anthony and Mary had been flashing in the semidarkness. Now the needles were still, as mother and sister leaned forward to listen to Susan. She said: "We can't all be nurses and go to the battlegrounds, like Mrs. Barton, but we can do more than knit socks. Socks are important for the soldiers, but we have to work with our brains, too, to force the congressmen to vote emancipation. So we are sending out a call for women from all over to meet at the Church of the Puritans in New York City and . . ."

She stopped. Something terrible and strange had happened. Daniel Anthony had been looking at her, smiling at her, when he had suddenly slumped down in his chair and the light had gone out of his face. Mrs. Anthony screamed.

Together the two sisters got the stricken man into bed, and Susan then hitched up horse and carriage and drove to Rochester for a doctor. He came, but it was no use.

Daniel Anthony lingered for a while, but there was never a doubt, and it was almost a relief when he died. The man lying in bed, suffering, moaning, was not the man they all knew; his passing was like an utter silence in the house. They all sat stunned. He had been husband and father, guide and helper, the one sure rock they could all lean on. Now he was gone.

Susan and Mary roused themselves first, in order to help

their grief-stricken mother. They conspired to keep her too busy to think. Would she do the cooking and baking for them while they wrote out the hundreds of letters for the call for women to meet in New York?

It did help Mrs. Anthony to look after and feed her two competent daughters. It healed her. Mary became Susan's secretary and combed through all the hundreds of names and addresses Susan had collected during her campaigning trips. Letters, appeals, invitations poured out of the Rochester farm to all over the state.

Then, with her mother's blessing, Susan went off to New York. Mrs. Anthony would be all right now. The farm was in her name and her husband had left her insurance. Mary was at home, working and contributing.

The Stantons had moved to New York because Henry Stanton had turned to newspaper work and become a battle correspondent for the *Tribune*. Susan went directly to their home, found a room in it for "Aunt Susan" and a letter waiting for her from Mr. Stanton.

Henry knew everything going on in Washington. He wrote Susan:

The country is rapidly going to destruction. The Army is in a state of mutiny for want of its pay and lack of a leader. Nothing can carry through but the Southern Negroes and nobody can marshall them into the struggle except the abolitionists.

Stanton was referring here to the arrogant resistance of Northern white military officers to letting Black men wear uniforms and serve as soldiers.

SUSAN B. ANTHONY

. . . the proclamation will be of no use to us if we are beaten and have a dissolution of the Union. Here then is work for you, Susan, put on your armor and go forth.

He knew Susan, and he knew his wife. Much as he loved and admired Elizabeth, he knew she did not have Susan's doggedness for hard, sustained work. Her mind darted here and there. Susan's stayed on a straight and level course.

If Northern women were to be marshaled to help, it was Susan who would get them.

The response to the call was wonderful. Women came to New York from many states. Lucy Stone came from Ohio; there was even a delegate from the territory of Wisconsin. To everyone's astonishment there were even white women and Black women with deep southern accents.

Out of the discussion at the Church of the Puritans came a proposal that they form the Women's National Loyal League. Susan put forth the resolution that the League would not accept any peace which did not include the full civil and political rights of all citizens, and that meant all Blacks and *all women*.

Some delegates objected to including woman suffrage in the resolution but the majority overruled them. Like Susan, the great majority considered woman's rights and Black rights as inseparable causes.

Because she knew the value of petitions Susan also proposed that the League institute a gigantic petition campaign. They would collect thousands and thousands of names for their resolutions and send them to congressmen and the federal government.

Mrs. Stanton was elected president of the League, and Susan was secretary. When the meeting was over and the last speech made and the women had gone back to their homes, it was Susan who had to "put on your armor and go forth."

She lived with the Stantons but rented Room 20 at Cooper Union. There she worked from early morning until late at night. She had a way of attracting volunteers. Young girls and their mothers reported to her office daily to send out letters and printed forms of the petitions; to answer the ever-increasing correspondence from abolitionists in small villages and big cities; and to help Susan get Mrs. Stanton's marvelous words to the newspapers.

Many did print what she had said, using her "Appeal" as the basis for editorials. It read:

> At this hour, the best word and work of every man and woman are imperatively demanded. To man . . . is assigned the forum, camp and field. What is woman's legitimate work, and how she may best accomplish it, is worthy of our earnest counsel with one another . . . a grand idea, such as freedom or justice, is needed to kindle and sustain the fires of a high enthusiasm!

And then followed the resolution of "no peace without full civil and political rights of all citizens."

A wealthy Bostonian, Charles F. Hovey, had left $50,000 in his will to be used "for the promotion of the antislavery cause and other reforms." Among the other reforms was the promotion of women's rights. The trustees were Wendell Phillips, William Lloyd Garrison, Parker Pillsbury, Abby Foster and several others, who were now so pleased with the women's League and Susan's all-out efforts that they paid her a twelve dollars per week salary.

It wasn't much but it helped. Susan wasn't living on the

Stanton's charity entirely. She wrote her mother that her lunch cost her five cents for strawberries, three cents for a glass of milk and five more cents for rusks—a kind of toasted bread.

Most of her salary she spent on office needs, especially postage. Henry Ward Beecher, a prominent minister, took up a collection for her work and raised $200, and a little more money trickled in from other supporters.

It wasn't long before the great numbers of women working to get petitions signed, the Appeal and the letters sent to President Lincoln, the stirring and awakening of Northern women to the principles of emancipation, began to make the male antislavery leaders sit up and take notice. When Susan asked Frederick Douglass and Wendell Phillips and others to come to Cooper Union and address meetings of women, they were glad to do so.

The audiences were surprisingly large. Susan and the other suffrage leaders were convincing women all over the North that they could do more than just roll bandages and knit socks to help win the war; they could also use their brains to help shape national policies.

It was a revolutionary idea but it caught fire. So many petitions were filled out and brought into Susan's office that she had to print new ones. As fast as they were filled she mailed them to the president and to congressmen. Washington sat up and took notice, too.

Susan knew she was doing a good job when Senator Charles Sumner offered to help with the financial burden of the postage. As a senator he had the right to frank his mail and send it free. He now mailed all her petitions under his own frank. Being against slavery himself, he was anxious to have his fellow congressmen persuaded to pass a constitutional amendment abolishing slavery, and Susan's petitions were excellent persuaders.

The opposition to emancipation, growing weaker in numbers, grew more violent in action. They went to the new poor emigrants to America, who had little or no understanding of the issues of the war, and said to them: Why should you have to fight and die for a Black? What is he to you?

The draft had been announced. There was grumbling against it. In the beginning of the war the Northern Army had been a volunteer one, but that simply had not worked out. Men had signed up for six months or a year and when their time was up they went home to their farms. No war could be fought that way. So the government had ordered a draft call.

Most men accepted it, even if they did not like it, but the poor European workers who had just arrived in New York were furious about it. They had one good reason. The rich could buy their way out of the draft by paying a substitute to fight—and perhaps to die—for them. The poor had to go. They had no choice.

Why did they have to go? Among people, many of whom did not even speak English and who had no idea of what Black slavery had meant, the word spread that they were being forced to go to war to free men who—as soon as they were free—would come to New York and take their jobs.

New York exploded into the shameful Draft Riots.

Susan was in her office when she heard the noise and the shouting. She ran down the hall to the doorway. Racing past her, filling the street from curb to curb, was a great mob of men shouting, "No draft!" and "Kill the niggers!" Some men were drunk. Others soon would be, because as the leaders swept by her, their followers took the chance to smash in the windows of a gin parlor and grab what bottles they could before running to catch up.

The mob was so maddened that it would have been at the cost of her life to go out and try to speak or reason with them. Susan went back to her office and told her women volunteers to stay where they were. Hopefully, the police would soon have the riot under control.

For a while this seemed to be so. The streets nearby were quiet. Henry Stanton managed to get to Cooper Union. But the news he brought Susan was worse than she had feared. The center of the riot was in the very area where the Stantons lived, at 75 West 45th Street, and he had not been able to get through to find out how his wife and children were.

The mob was out of control. They had found an orphanage for Black children near the Stanton home. Reports were that some of the children had been killed. Certainly Black men had died all over the city, wherever the mob had found them.

Henry Stanton's life was in danger. The drunken rioters identified Horace Greeley and his *Tribune* and his writers—such as Stanton—as high on the list of their enemies and they were looking for the newspapermen. Nevertheless, Stanton and Susan decided to try their luck at reaching home. If Mrs. Stanton and the children were under attack they wanted to share their danger.

As Susan followed Henry she could hear yells far off, but the streets through which they walked were deserted. The people were inside, with the doors closed and the shutters pulled to. Broken glass littered the ground in front of stores and taverns; the mob had turned to looting.

Fortunately, just as Susan and Henry Stanton turned into 45th Street, there was a favorable turn in the struggle, and the police for once got the upper hand and chased the mob out of the area. Henry hammered on his door and it was un-bolted; he and Susan dashed inside.

They found intrepid little Elizabeth Cady Stanton armed with a stick and standing guard at the foot of the staircase, ready to hit anyone who would try to go up and get her children. It was quickly decided that the whole family should get out of the house now, while they had the chance. The street and the area was too dangerous to stay in, if the mob should form again and come back.

Susan held the hands of Margaret and Theodore Stanton, while Mrs. Stanton took two other children and Mr. Stanton carried the smaller ones, and they made their way through back streets and alleys until they reached the home of Dr. Bayard, Elizabeth's brother-in-law. Horace Greeley had already taken refuge there. The grown-ups spent the long, hideous night listening to the screams of victims and the hoarse, animal shouting of the mob as it once more got out of control and rampaged through New York.

When the riots were finally over, the cost in human lives and property was horrible. Blacks had been strung up to lampposts; whole families had been burned to death. White Abolitionist leaders had been mauled and injured and their homes destroyed. The *Tribune* office was wrecked.

Yet the draft went on and the war continued. There was no question but that the riot mob had been small in number and not representative of the general feeling in the North. The actions of the mob had been frightful, but they had been motivated by fear, ignorance and prejudice, and by the anger over the buying of substitutes.

Susan settled back to work. By the end of the year she had gathered one hundred thousand signatures to her petition; within a few months more she had four hundred thousand!

Senator Sumner and Wendell Phillips and the others could not praise her efforts highly enough. There was no doubt, they said, but that the women's league was influencing the votes.

The Senate passed the Thirteenth Amendment in April, 1864. There was simply no question now but that the House of Representatives would follow suit and the abolition of slavery would become part of the Constitution.

The petition campaign was over, and Susan went home to Rochester. Once again she had time to think of her future, while her hands were busy with the kitchen and house.

The family now accepted the fact that Susan would only be a visitor, and would always be needed somewhere else, as a leader in national social issues. However, the closeness of the Anthonys would always include her. Mrs. Anthony and Mary had stayed with the farm for the time being, Guelma and her husband were near and now Hannah and Eugene Mosher moved to Rochester. The big event though was Daniel, Jr.'s, marriage.

He had served well in the Army. When his volunteer regiment was disbanded he had returned to Leavenworth and to his newspaper, the Leavenworth *Times,* had been elected mayor of the town and, having reached the age of forty, had proposed to Miss Anna Osborne, a very beautiful and well-educated woman from Martha's Vineyard, Massachusetts. The wedding took place at the Rochester farm in January, 1864.

Susan worked hard to make the wedding a lovely one. Once again she was happy baking and cooking and sewing, but her thoughts were of what she would do next.

The league would be disbanded. It had served its special purpose of arousing women to the real issues of the war and getting them to support full emancipation. The league's role in pushing the vote through Congress had been a big one.

Susan did not doubt that the North would finally win the war. Lincoln had been reelected. The Army was a real one now. Victories were on the increase. Without support from abroad, the South did not have the economy to last out much longer.

One part of Susan's mind rejoiced over this; the other part felt let down and confused. After such strenuous activity she was empty, unused, unwanted. The war occupied everyone's thoughts. No one cared at the moment about woman suffrage. William Lloyd Garrison was even talking about disbanding the Antislavery League, since it had accomplished its purpose in the Thirteenth Amendment.

Susan was out of a job and had no money of her own. Mrs. Anthony decided to sell the farm. She and Mary would move into Guelma's house temporarily. Of course Susan was welcome, but she hated charity, even from her family. For a little while no one thought of that, because Guelma's daughter, Ann Eliza, suddenly died, and the McLeans were more than glad to have Susan there to nurse Guelma through her grief.

But soon Susan felt herself to be just a guest, living off her family and eating their food and contributing nothing. At this moment Daniel, Jr., wrote her from Kansas that he truly did need her to help him run his newspaper.

She went immediately. Leavenworth was growing into a bustling city. Susan worked hard and learned the newspaper business and loved it, although brother Daniel would not let her write his editorials. They were too inflammatory, he declared, for a businessman determined to make his paper big and prosperous. Still, she might have stayed on in Kansas, earning a decent living and doing little else, but once again life caught her up and flung her out.

The war had ended. The country had lived through the shock of Abraham Lincoln's assassination. Now unity between North and South was once again being knitted together, although in pain and turmoil and confusion. It was necessary now for Congress to pass another amendment. The first had given freedom; this one would give the vote.

Susan was sitting in the newspaper office in Kansas clipping out items of news from other newspapers, when her eye fell upon a report from Washington on the proposed writing of the amendment which would become the Fourteenth.

She read and gasped. The amendment would give the right of the vote to the emancipated slaves—but only to males. That designation "male" had never before been used in the Constitution. The Constitution had used *person* or *citizen;* it had never used the word *male.* The new wording was deliberately aimed, Susan knew, to stop the progress of woman suffrage. White men and Black men would be able to vote, but white women—and Black women—would not.

In the flash of an instant she made up her mind. She must again "put on her armor and go forth." Surely such men as Wendell Phillips and Frederick Douglass and William Lloyd Garrison and Horace Greeley would rally around the women to see that this monstrous injustice did not pass. She quit her job and headed East.

Chapter Seven

Before Susan left Kansas she had written Wendell Phillips, and his answer waited for her in Rochester. His letter said nothing about woman suffrage, but he told her that, unlike William Lloyd Garrison, he did not think the job was finished. Getting the Fourteenth Amendment passed would not be much easier than getting the Thirteenth.

He needed her. He needed her powerful support for Black suffrage. Would she help?

She barely had time to greet her family before she was off again on a whirlwind tour, following her old campaign route throughout New York, speaking everywhere for suffrage. But she did have time to correspond with Mrs. Stanton, and the two of them arranged a Woman's Rights Convention for the following May, 1866.

As soon as her lecture tour was over Susan was back in the Stanton home in New York.

The two women worked out a plan which seemed to them logical, practical and fair. The old Antislavery Society people, abandoned by Garrison, and the Woman's Rights Association should merge into one American Equal Rights Association which would fight for suffrage for the Black and for women.

They presented their idea to Wendell Phillips. To Susan's

surprise he seemed hesitant. He was carrying on the Anti-slavery Society, and he claimed it would require a three-months' notice sent out to all its members to change its name and character. That was in its charter.

"Very well," said Susan, "that can easily be done. We have three months before May. Your convention is to be held then; so is ours. The conventions can be held in New York one after the other. The proposal can be made to both. Then we can reconvene as one association."

What made it seem even more simple to her was that the membership of both was made up of many of the same people. The same men and women had belonged to both in the past; now they would be one.

May came and Susan was on the speaker's platform of the Antislavery Society. She made the motion. "I hereby propose that this Society be disbanded and join with the Woman's Rights group to form one American Equal Rights Association, for suffrage for all."

The tall, elegant Wendell Phillips rose and declared her out of order. She stared at him in astonishment. "Why?" she asked. The whole audience stirred uneasily and murmurs ran through the hall.

"Because no notice was sent out, as is required by our constitution," he declared.

"Why was it not sent out? Who countermanded your order?" she asked.

"I did." Wendell Phillips then rapped for silence and went smoothly on with the next point of business. Susan sank back in her chair, stunned. She glanced at Mrs. Stanton whose face was as astounded as her own.

There was no time to ask why—not then. Phillips disappeared as soon as the meeting was over, and both women had to prepare for the Woman's Rights Convention the next day.

The absence of Wendell Phillips and most other male supporters at that meeting was noticeable. Nevertheless, the women went ahead and voted the change of name, and the broadening of the character of their organization to the fight for suffrage beyond their own.

On the morning following, Susan and Mrs. Stanton came face to face with Wendell Phillips in the newspaper office of the *Antislavery Standard*. They still felt he must have had some good reason for having let them down; in fact they could not believe he had. There had to have been some mistake.

"Why?" Susan asked again. "Why did you agree and then countermand your order?"

Phillips was an eloquent and suave speaker. He paid them both great compliments, but he was sorry—the time was not yet ripe for woman suffrage. This was the Black's "hour." They must not confuse the issue. They must not put forth their own demands when it might result in giving congressmen an excuse not to give the vote to Blacks.

"Everyone must make sacrifices," he reminded them kindly. As for the wording of the Fourteenth Amendment, "The question of striking out the word 'male,' " said Phillips, "we shall of course present as an intellectual theory, but not as a practical thing. . . ."

Mrs. Stanton was nodding her head. Phillips' great charm and persuasive voice had wrought a spell upon her. But not upon Susan. She was furious. The whole thing was a betrayal. She faced him squarely and raised her hand. "I would sooner cut off my right hand than ask for the ballot for the Black man and not for women."

As she stormed out she heard Mrs. Stanton exclaim, "Why, I never knew Susan Anthony could be so rude!"

Desolate, Susan walked for hours, trying to calm herself, trying to overcome the deep hurt. Since she was a young woman she had admired, even revered, the great Wendell Phillips. She had gone anywhere he had asked her to, undertaken any task he had asked of her, suffered any hardship. He had been the leader. How proud she had been when her work had been good enough to place her on committees with him! How many times had she, and other women, given up speaking for woman's rights in order to speak for the Antislavery Society!

Now she and other women were to be told they must step aside—this was not their "hour!"

How could Mrs. Stanton have agreed with him?

Exhausted at last and too tired to think any more, Susan went to the Stanton house and quietly let herself in with her own key. It was late. She hoped they were all asleep.

But Mrs. Stanton was waiting for her, wide awake, and with signs of tears on her face. She threw herself at Susan, crying: "I never was so glad to see you! Do tell me what is the matter with me. I feel as if I had been scourged from the crown of my head to the soles of my feet!"

Mrs. Stanton was shocked at herself. No sooner had she reached home and escaped from the charm and magnetism of Wendell Phillips than the full import of what she had done hit her. He was wrong and she had supported him. Susan was right and she had deserted her. How could she?

Susan wasted no time reproaching her. Late that night and all the next day they talked the matter over with Henry Stanton. Wendell Phillips' attitude explained so much that had been puzzling them. It explained why so many of their male members of the Woman's Rights Convention had stayed

112

away: they had not wanted to vote for an association working for both Black and woman suffrage.

It explained why their old supporters in Congress, Thaddeus Stevens and Senator Sumner, had refused to present the signatures Susan had gotten.

Was Phillips right, the women asked themselves. Would a campaign to strike out the word "male" from the new amendment prevent the amendment from passing Congress?

"Nonsense," said Susan. "If the Constitution had said *male* before there would be some excuse, but at this moment we are only asking that this amendment conform to the usual wording: citizen or person. It is being deliberately inserted against us. If they let that stand, our so-called friends are working to push us backwards. They are stepping on us to get what they want."

What hurt Susan most was that Frederick Douglass, of all people, had vehemently sided with the other men. Couldn't he see how wrong it was that Black men, and not Black women, should get the vote?

How often he had spoken to Susan, reverently, of the bravery and leadership of Black women! There was Harriet Tubman, who had escaped to freedom and then risked that freedom and her very life to go back to the South over and over and lead slaves North through the underground railway. There was Sojourner Truth, whose powerful, brilliant, untutored mind swept audiences into a fervor against slavery. And what of his own wife, Anna?

Perhaps Susan was a little harsh in her judgment. Frederick Douglass saw that the government had no real plan to help the emancipated slaves or straighten out the chaos in the South. He feared—and with reason—that they might lose almost everything they had fought for. He grabbed for any solid victory quickly, before everything was swept away again.

In the next months Susan and Mrs. Stanton felt very much alone in their new organization. Not only had most of the men antislavery leaders deserted them, but so had many women.

Of all the prominent figures among the men, only Parker Pillsbury, the big, black-bearded man from New Hampshire who had left the ministry to work full-time against slavery, changed his mind and told Wendell Phillips he was wrong. Pillsbury came to Susan to declare himself on her side. He encouraged her to stand up and fight wherever she could.

Kansas had placed on its state ballot the two issues: the vote for Blacks and the vote for women. As soon as Mrs. Stanton and Susan heard of this they wrote to Lucy Stone and her husband, Henry Blackwell, asking them to campaign in Kansas for the next two months. This would give Susan the chance to raise money for herself and Mrs. Stanton to go to Kansas for the last, decisive autumn months of the campaign.

Wendell Phillips refused to give them a penny from the Hovey Fund, although the donor had specifically asked that woman suffrage be included when the money was distributed. Susan had to walk from house to house of every possible friend or supporter and beg for donations for the trip. Mrs. Stanton was busy making arrangements for the care of her family while she was away.

Once they arrived in Kansas they found an inexpensive office room in Lawrence, and a few volunteers to come in and answer mail and send out pamphlets. Then Mrs. Stanton headed one way, in a carriage drawn by mules, and escorted by a man who was an old friend and supporter of woman's rights. Susan went the other way, getting along as best she could.

All along the back country, up and down lanes to farms and homestead cabins, into small villages, fording rivers where there were no bridges, getting mired ankle-deep in mud, soaked in rain and blistered by the sun, the two women went on their campaign. They talked to farmers and farmers' wives who had not seen a neighbor in weeks, and were glad to have them stop for the night. They handed out pamphlets and had to read them aloud to illiterate families. They talked and argued and reasoned. They spoke to one man in a whole morning or to hundreds in an evening.

Sometimes they ran into hostility and meanness. "Sooner let my old mule vote than my old woman," said one man, spitting tobacco juice on Mrs. Stanton's dress. Another shook his fist at Susan. "You tryin' to tell me a man what was a black slave goin' to have a vote good as mine? You git outa here, woman!"

The traveling, accommodations and threats were harder on Mrs. Stanton than they were on Susan. Elizabeth Cady was a dainty woman in her personal habits: she had always had plenty of warm water and fine soap for her daily bath. She was accustomed to changing from morning to afternoon dresses, or from housedresses to street wear. She was proud of her soft, white curly hair and the way it looked under her immaculate white lace bonnets.

What she found in country inns were hard beds and cold water and soap that did not lather, and a small basin out of which she had to try to get herself clean all over. She learned, as Susan had long ago, that no matter how tired she was at night she had to clean spots off her suits or dress, clean and polish her shoes, beg a pressing iron off the kitchen stove and do all this herself if she was to be presentable the next day.

Mrs. Stanton was plump but the extra pounds did not seem to help a bit to ease the jouncing, jolting, weary rides each day. All that kept her going sometimes was the knowledge that Susan was going through the same hardships. If Susan would not quit, neither would she.

The Republican Party clubs in each town were supposed to help the women. A few did, but most did not. The party that had been born and which had elected its first president on a platform opposing slavery was now quickly losing its idealism and becoming big and powerful—and ready to compromise for votes for its politicians.

Time was pressing. Susan's money, doled out between the two of them, was running out and it was still only September. Voting day was not until November. Susan came back to the Lawrence office, hoping to find letters with checks in them. There were none.

She was sitting there, her elbows on the desk and her head in her hands, trying to think of a way out, when there was a knock on the door and a man entered. He would have been a striking-looking individual in any place, but in that drab, plainly-furnished room he looked like a peacock in a barnyard.

"Miss Anthony? I knew you from your pictures." Carefully he took off his elegant kid gloves, put them and his hat and gold-knobbed cane on her desk. "I am George Francis Train. I have come to give you my financial support and enlist as a speaker in your cause." He smiled, showing a superb confidence in himself that kept her speechless for a moment. "Together, you and I, Miss Anthony, will sweep the voters off their feet."

If it hadn't been for his unmistakable New England voice, she might have thought him a foreigner because of his olive complexion and dark, curly hair and his extremely fashionable clothes, so unfitted to Kansas. But she knew he was from New England not only from his voice, but because she already knew a lot—from gossip and newspapers—about George Francis Train.

He was only thirty-eight, but he had already made a small fortune. He could have made a huge one, but he just could not stay put in one business enterprise for very long before giving it up and darting to another.

He had helped to form a corporation, the Crédit Mobilier, which had financed the Union Pacific Railway in the stretch between Nebraska and Utah, opening up that part of the West. He had been given much land along the railway right of way and had laid out towns and sold lots. When they did not sell as fast as he would have liked, he sold out carelessly—leaving others to follow behind and reap great profits from his work.

He didn't care. He wanted a new interest. Evidently here, in this shabby little office, talking to the shabbily-dressed, forty-seven-year-old spinster Susan B. Anthony, he thought he had found it.

"You," she finally managed to say, "want to canvass the state for votes for Blacks?"

"For votes for *women!*" he exploded. "For the Black, yes, if you wish, but my real interest is in seeing women justified, women rising to their full potentials, women in high office—which can only be done by women voting. Miss Anthony, listen to me . . ." and for a half hour he paced her office, spouting such a lavish flow of words as she had never heard before. Dazed, she could only catch a word or a phrase now and then: "the brains of half the human race treated as if they were children," ". . . put matters right . . . ," ". . . should have every legal privilege of a man . . ." What Susan was really thinking of was when would be the quickest that Mrs. Stanton could reach Lawrence.

They had to talk this over. George Francis Train had put one hundred dollars on Susan's desk, as if it was nothing. This she could accept, but did they want him for a speaker? Fortunately, Elizabeth Cady Stanton drove in two days later and met Train.

They got along well from the very start. Even though she was now fifty years old, Mrs. Stanton was still conscious of being pretty, and Train liked her charming ways, her clothes and her witty way of speaking. Mrs. Stanton urged Susan to include him as a campaigner.

Susan agreed. She mapped out a week's tour for him, including what roads he was to take, what farms he was to visit and what meetings she had already set up for afternoon and evening speeches. She had originally planned it for herself, but this would give her a chance to stay in Lawrence and see to the printing of more pamphlets and writing of more letters.

It also gave her a chance to see Merritt and his wife and babies. She had last seen him when she had come to work in Daniel, Jr.'s, newspaper office, when Merritt was just out of the army, looking gaunt and war-weary. Now she was pleased to see that he was well and happy.

Only three days of the week had elapsed when George Francis Train came back to Lawrence and into the office.

"Why are you here?" demanded Susan, looking up from her pile of correspondence.

"Why? Do you realize that not one of those towns where you scheduled meetings is on the railroad? I would have had to take wagons or hire a carriage—and those roads! By the time I arrived I was covered with dust and dirt. I was ashamed to go on the platform looking less than a gentleman."

"Then," said Susan, getting up, "I shall have to go in your place, even if I look less than a lady."

"You can't!"

"I can and must. I have been doing that, and even much worse, for years. If you will not appear at those meetings I shall have to go, even if I must drive a carriage all night, all alone. Those meetings have been announced and scheduled; we must never fail an audience."

Train looked steadily at her for a long moment and she gave him a composed and determined look in return. Then he picked up his hat. "I believe you would go. I believe you would drive all night. Forgive me, Miss Anthony, for under-estimating you. I will never do it again. And I will finish the tour."

He gave her a quick grin, a salute and was off.

From that moment, much as he still liked Mrs. Stanton and appreciated her, Susan was the one he admired the most and acknowledged as the head of their crusade. It was to her he went for instructions; it was from her he would—usually—take orders.

His arrival made all the difference in their campaign. He was generous with the money they needed so much. He was a marvelous speaker. Being of Irish ancestry and having been around Irish railroad workers he knew just how to talk to the large number of Irishmen who were moving into Kansas and who would have a vote. They were, for the most part, prejudiced against Blacks and had no good opinion of women's minds, but George Francis Train could laugh and coax and tease them out of their prejudices.

He made a great point out of comparing the Irishman's desire for freedom from England to the desire for freedom on the part of women. The Irish were denied their rights; so were all women. Then, when his speech got too serious and heated, he would make a joke and his audience would roar with laughter.

The vote of the Irish in November for suffrage for Blacks and for women was astoundingly high. No one had expected that.

No one had expected that there would be nine thousand votes for woman suffrage and ten thousand for Black suffrage, as the total, out of a state vote of thirty thousand, in that year of 1867. Kansas had been the scene of bitter conflict. Kansas was sick of hearing about the rights of Black men—so Susan had been warned. The Republican Party had done little to help and often had tried to keep those "meddling females" from stirring up controversy.

Yet suffrage had rolled up high votes. Since the strength of the vote for Black suffrage and for woman suffrage was almost the same, it seemed proof to Susan, Mrs. Stanton and Mr. Train that the position of such men as Wendell Phillips was utter nonsense. Campaigning for both causes had hurt neither one.

George Francis Train had nothing but scorn for Phillips. During one speech in the Kansas campaign when he was addressing a group of woman's rights supporters he had said:

Where is Wendell Phillips today? Where is William

Lloyd Garrison? Not one of their (Susan and Mrs. Stanton's) old army generals at hand; nobody but that wonderful, eccentric, independent, extraordinary genius and political reformer of America, who is sweeping off all the politicians before him like a hurricane, your modest friend, the future President of America, George Francis Train!

Everyone laughed, but Susan was embarrassed. It must surely be just a joke, yet she knew that Train was such a strange mixture of half-genius, half-madcap that he might just possibly think of himself as a future presidential candidate. She put the thought aside. She had something much more real to consider.

Train had found out that her secret dream was to have a newspaper for the Equal Rights Society. He had immediately said: "I will give you the money," and that night he had announced at a public meeting that a woman's rights newspaper would be published shortly from New York, with Mrs. Stanton as editor, and Susan B. Anthony in charge of all.

Its motto, he declared, would be: "Men, their rights, and nothing more; women, their rights, and nothing less," and the name of the paper would be the *Revolution*.

Giving neither Susan nor Elizabeth Cady time to think or object, he took them on a great speaking tour homeward, going from one great city to another, traveling in the most luxurious style, staying in the finest hotels. They were dazzled.

They also had a chance to talk to women in Chicago, St. Louis, Cincinnati, Cleveland and Louisville, as well as the big eastern cities. It was a great opportunity to stir interest in local chapters of the Equal Rights Society, and to get subscriptions for the *Revolution*.

Susan stopped off in Rochester. She found that her mother had decided to buy a home for herself and Mary inside the city of Rochester. Two fairly large brick homes, of ten to twelve rooms each, were for sale, side by side. Mrs. Anthony bought one, and Hannah and Eugene Mosher bought the other. Mrs. Anthony's was large enough so she could ask Guelma and Aaron and their two children to come and live with her. The family was close once more, and there was a room reserved for Susan.

She had no time to sleep in it more than one night, however. She rushed on to New York. Both she and George Francis Train were fast workers; both could be ruthless in overcoming delays. There was no lack of money to get things started, and by January 8, 1868, the first copy of the *Revolution* was on the newsstands.

It was a fine newspaper, excellently written. In addition to Mrs. Stanton's clever remarks about politics and politicians, Parker Pillsbury had come onto the staff as coeditor. He had become so indignant when Phillips had withheld the Hovey money from Susan that he had offered his services for the *Revolution,* which were gladly accepted. He was a good balance for Mrs. Stanton and his articles were thoughtful and soundly written—even beautifully written.

Almost all of the paper dealt with woman suffrage and the terrible wreck of Reconstruction in the aftermath of the war. No amount of constitutional amendments could free the Black people so long as whites were encouraged to use terror and murder and the threat of starvation against them. The bonds were still there.

No real plans had been made to educate Black men and women, or to give them jobs away from the plantations. Every effort was made to keep them in subjugation. This was the very thing Susan B. Anthony had warned about years ago at meetings, after she had listened to Frederick Douglass' concern.

The *Revolution* was filled with news stories and editorials dealing with equal rights, but space was also given for a column by George Francis Train. This seemed only fair to Susan, since he had put up the money to start the paper.

In his column he came out in favor of paper money, favored by Western money interests, but hated by the big Eastern financiers. He was also a Democrat and liked to be sarcastic about the Republican Party.

None of these financial or political matters meant much to Susan or the editors. They thought Train's column unimportant. But their former friends did not think so. They were furious. They were outraged. They were highly disgusted with Susan B. Anthony, Mrs. Elizabeth Cady Stanton, Parker Pillsbury—and they said so. While most of the indignation centered around Train, it soon became evident to Susan and to Elizabeth Cady that they were being criticized or snubbed because they had dared to do something without the advice of the men who thought they had put both women firmly in their place.

Horace Greeley of the *Tribune* loftily ignored the new newspaper. The *New York Times,* edited by Henry J. Raymond, made fun of it in an editorial:

It is out at last. If the women, as a body, have not succeeded in getting up a revolution, Susan B. Anthony, as their representative, has. Her *Revolution* was issued last Thursday as a sort of New York's gift to what she considered a yearning public. . . . If Mrs. Stanton would attend a little more to her domestic duties and a little less to those of the great public, perhaps she would exalt her sex quite as much as she does by quixotically fighting windmills . . . (woman) best honors herself and her sex by leaving public affairs behind her, and by endeavoring to show how happy she can make the little world of which she has just become the brilliant center.

Ever since she had been a young woman and had heard her father speak reverently of William Lloyd Garrison, ever since she had read his great and ringing calls for abolition in his *Liberator,* she had loved and admired him as one of the most magnificent Americans. Now he sent her a letter. Sorrowfully, she printed it in the next issue of the *Revolution:*

Dear Miss Anthony: In all friendliness and with the highest regard for the Woman's Rights movement, I can not refrain from expressing my regret and astonishment that you and Mrs. Stanton should have taken such leave of good sense, and departed so far from true self-respect, as to be travelling companions and associate lecturers with that crack-brained harlequin and semi-lunatic, George Francis Train! You may, if you choose, denounce Henry Ward Beecher and Wendell Phillips (the two ablest advocates of Woman's Rights on this side of the Atlantic) and swap them off for the nondescript Train; but, in thus doing, you will only subject yourselves to merited ridicule and condemnation, and turn the movement which you aim to promote into unnecessary contempt.

That was only part of it. The rest was the same—a scolding of the women and a blast at Train. Garrison seemed particularly upset at Train's links with Western money rather than Eastern Wall Street.

The next incident occurred at an antislavery festival party. Mr. and Mrs. Stanton went to it, as they always did. Elizabeth was conversing in a group which included Wendell Phillips. Mr. Phillips' niece, seeing that he resolutely paid no attention to Mrs. Stanton, pulled at his sleeve and said: "Uncle, this is *Mrs. Stanton,*" thinking he had not noticed his old friend. Elizabeth heard her and came forward, holding out her hand, at which Phillips put both his hands behind his back and turned away. It was a deliberate snub.

Both Susan and Elizabeth were past the stage of being hurt. Susan was boiling mad.

No one had to tell her that George Francis Train was odd and had freak enthusiasms. She had to deal with them. But at least he did not patronize her. He had tried to help her. Those other great men were paying nothing but lip service to woman's rights.

It was clear to her that they were willing to help women just so long as they could lead and women would do as they said. Suffrage had to come eventually, slowly, and it had to come *their* way. "Stuff and nonsense!" exclaimed Susan.

At forty-seven years of age she was finding that she had outgrown all timidity. She was tart and outspoken and full of the juice of independence.

Let those others say whatever they liked, she had a newspaper! She had the *Revolution.* It was hers. Pillsbury and Mrs. Stanton kept it a fresh, readable and interesting paper, but Susan kept it going. Without her ability to run it and pay for it, it would have been a failure.

SUSAN B. ANTHONY

This was particularly so when George Francis Train appeared in the newspaper office on Park Avenue one day and told her, as casually as if he were going to New Jersey, that he was taking off for Ireland and might not be back for six months. He had a new cause, that of the Irish national movement for freedom from England. He wished Susan good luck, left her six hundred dollars and vanished.

For a long time she just sat and looked at the check, and then glanced around the office. Figures clicked in her brain: so much for printing, paper, supplies, for all the hundred and one expenses. Six hundred dollars was nothing; it would not last any time at all. Somehow she would have to find the money for the newspaper, and she would have to do it all by herself.

For now Train was gone. Hers was the final say about everything.

She was going to have to work harder than she ever had in her whole life, and she had never been happier.

Chapter Eight

Like her two tough-minded grandmothers, Susan B. Anthony was never happier than when she was running things, creating things and doing what seemed to be the impossible. She had learned the basics of operating a newspaper by working for her brother, but there were new tasks now that the *Revolution* was all her own.

She marched into shops, fighting her way past assistants to see the boss and sell him on putting an advertisement in her paper. She took bundles of the *Revolution,* right off the press, around to various newsvendors on New York streets and got them to handle it along with their regular papers.

Copies were mailed to their few subscribers and sent free to every influential citizen, politician or other newspaper. It was a boost for the *Revolution* when some other paper quoted a news item or an editorial of Parker Pillsbury's or Mrs. Stanton's.

Susan also meddled with her two editors.

It was she who brought up the problems of working girls. It started when she got a letter in her morning mail one day from a Jennie Collins who was leading a strike against a spinning mill in Dover, New Hampshire. The letter explained the strike: ". . . two looms was a girl's work. Then they reduced their wages and added another loom. Again they cut down and added still another loom . . . now a girl's work is six and seven looms."

Seven looms! Susan knew from her own father's factory that seven looms would be incredibly hard on a girl's health. Her eyes and fingers could not stand the strain of such hard, fast work—and at cut wages, too!

Miss Collins had added in her letter that there were now forty-eight thousand factory girls in Massachusetts, alone.

The *Revolution* printed that letter and every other one that came from factory girls; the editors and Susan encouraged them to write in and tell their stories.

"It's about time," declared Susan, "that America wakes up to the fact that females aren't the sheltered, protected little darlings men like to think they are!"

Of course, the main part of the newspaper was devoted to pressure against the passage of the Fourteenth and Fifteenth Amendments, in the way they were now written. The *Revolution* had no quarrel with section one of the Fourteenth which began: "All persons born or naturalized in the United States, and subject to the jurisdiction thereof, are citizens of the United States and of the State wherein they reside. . . ."

Well and good! "All persons" could certainly be interpreted as women, too. It was the wording of section two which said: ". . . when the right to vote at any election . . . is denied to any of the male inhabitants of such State. . . ." and followed with the penalty for such denial, that brought forth one stinging, indignant editorial after another. All to no avail. The Fourteenth Amendment was ratified by the states in July, 1868, and the Fifteenth on March 30, 1870.

The *Revolution* had been almost the only forceful voice

in America pointing out the deliberate unfairness to women in both amendments. The woman's rights movement and its leaders were split and ineffectual.

Lucy Stone had made it clear she would have nothing to do with Susan B. Anthony, Mrs. Stanton, their newspaper or their crazy friend, Mr. Train. For a while it seemed as if all the other women leaders would side with Lucy, but it was only that many of them had to have time to sit down and think and make up their minds. Then the great Lucretia Mott declared that Susan and Elizabeth Cady Stanton were right and she was with them. The renowned Lydia Maria Child, novelist and pioneer writer of antislavery tracts—a woman before whom even Wendell Phillips bowed—asked to become a member of Susan's organization. Most of the Boston women and men, however, clung to Phillips and Lucy Stone, who had moved back there from Ohio.

Susan's Equal Rights Society changed to the National Suffrage Association; the Bostonians formed the American Suffrage Association. During these dismal times when it seemed as if nobody could do anything but make petty, nasty remarks about people who had once been their friends, Susan's newspaper was the only really alive, penetrating, powerful speaker for suffrage.

Then the American Suffrage Association decided to publish its own newspaper: the *Woman's Journal*. It was well-financed, solidly backed and Lucy Stone was a capable editor. The newspaper strongly advocated that women advance by training for professions and educating themselves. It did not bother senators with petitions; it did not champion working women who were striking for higher wages; it did not annoy anyone. With its first issue on January 8, 1870, it was a success, and it killed the *Revolution*. There simply were not enough supporters who would subscribe to two woman's rights newspapers.

For Susan the blow was staggering. All the businessmen who refused advertising to her because she championed women workers went to the new *Woman's Journal*. It had style and charm. Subscribers could comfort themselves in knowing that they need not go out and challenge state or national governments; the emphasis now was on an individual struggle to get a girl into a college.

Advice from the *Woman's Journal* to women was the same as what was given to the Blacks: first raise yourself to equality before demanding it—which was said while the white male rulers of the country kept their heels firmly planted on the necks of the subjected.

Susan and the *Revolution* had been in financial debt almost from the beginning, in spite of all she could do. George Francis Train had returned from Ireland (where he had been in jail as a rebel), but he was losing his money faster than he acquired it, and could give her no help.

A Mrs. Bullard, who wanted to try her hand at editing, paid Susan one dollar for all the office property. When Mrs. Stanton and Parker Pillsbury walked out the door for the last time it was with sadness; when Susan walked out it was with a staggering debt of ten thousand dollars.

She didn't complain. It was only fair. She was the proprietor; she had taken on the responsibility, knowing what she was doing; she had kept going when common sense told her to stop; now she had to pay her debts.

The worst thing of all, however, was to see the *Woman's Journal* flourishing. In its pages she could read exactly why she and Lucy Stone—much as they sincerely respected each other's abilities—could not agree. The backers of the paper were some of the leading Massachusetts figures of the Republican Party, and it was rumored that the *Journal* had promised not to mention votes for women as an "immediate issue," which would have embarrassed the Republican Party.

Susan could not compromise with this attitude. She was without any political affiliation at all, and didn't trust a single politician. She tried to wish the *Journal* well in its sedate approach to slow reforms; then she turned her back on it and went to work.

That money had to be paid back. The only way Susan could do it was by lecturing and charging for her lectures. To her amazement she found herself greatly in demand and able to charge from $50 to $150 for a single speech. At that rate it wouldn't be many years before she was free of debt.

Susan had given up the *Revolution* in June, but something had happened in February which proved to be an enormous help. On the 15th she had her fiftieth birthday. The women closest to her started plans for a party; it grew into a great demonstration and celebration. Susan B. Anthony discovered that she was famous.

Newspapers carried kind or not-so-kind stories about her, but few ignored her, whether in New York, Washington, Philadelphia or Cincinnati. Presents poured in and she had no false pride about accepting a silk dress from Anna Dickinson, or all the checks from ten to fifty dollars. Letters and telegrams came from old friends and even from strangers.

She wrote in her diary that night after the festivities: "Fiftieth birthday! One half-century done, one score of it hard labor for bettering humanity—oh, such a struggle!"

But her struggle was not over; it was only beginning. She did not think of herself as old. Her birthday had made her news and that was what counted, since it greatly helped her get speaking dates. She took every one that came along, to slice a few more dollars off her debt, and only stopped for a brief visit home now and then or a National Suffrage Convention in Washington, D. C.

In Washington she met a few new congressmen who were favorable to woman suffrage: Wade from Ohio, Pomeroy from Kansas and a few others. On March 15, 1869, George W. Julian of Indiana had introduced a resolution in Congress proposing a sixteenth amendment to the Constitution which would give women the vote.

Susan, Mrs. Stanton and other suffrage leaders were pondering what method was best. Should it be an all-out effort for a sixteenth amendment? Susan slightly favored that. But there was also the possibility of getting suffrage state by state; Wyoming had taken the whole nation by complete surprise in deciding that its women had an equal vote and ballot with its men.

Then there was a third method: to challenge the Fourteenth Amendment and go to the polls under its first section, disregarding its second section.

No matter which way it came about, the theme of Susan's talks was "The Power of the Ballot" and the right of women to vote. She spoke so well, to so many audiences, that she had paid back sixteen hundred dollars of her debt by the end of 1870.

Mrs. Stanton was also lecturing—from necessity. The days of the Cady money were gone; both she and her husband had so selflessly devoted themselves to abolition and woman's rights they had neglected their own finances. Henry Stanton was doing the best he could now as a part-time lawyer and part-time newspaper reporter, but the education of six chil-

dren was costly, and Elizabeth Cady Stanton had to earn
money for the first time in her life.

When lecture dates in California were offered, both women
jumped at the chance. All along the way, in Wyoming and
Utah and elsewhere, they stopped to make speeches, and
wound up a successful tour in California by going on to
Oregon and Washington.

If they were earning money they were also making new
friends for the woman's rights movement, and meeting some
wonderful workers such as Abigail Scott Duniway, the pioneer
suffrage leader in Oregon.

On New Year's Eve, 1871, while the train sped eastwards
towards home, Susan wrote in her diary that she had earned
a profit of $2,271 that year towards paying the debts of the
Revolution. Would she ever get it all paid? How many more
lecture tours, traveling in sticky summer heat or winter
blizzards, must she make before she was free and clear again?

In the spring of 1872 she was traveling, talking, lecturing
all through Kansas and Nebraska, which at least gave her the
chance to visit a while with both Merritt and Daniel, Jr.,
and their families. This time Mrs. Stanton was not with her;
they were on separate lecture circuits.

Eighteen seventy-two was an election campaign year for
the president of the United States, and the nation was in an
uproar over it. The Democrats nominated Charles O'Conor;
the Republicans renominated Grant for a second term; and
the Liberal Republicans chose Horace Greeley to oppose
Grant because of the corruption of the past four years.

Susan B. Anthony was not a delegate; she was not a voter;
she belonged to no party, but she went to every state convention of all three groups, whenever she could. And she

rose to demand that each one put a plank in its campaign program for votes for women.

Astonishingly, when she attended the Republican Party convention in Philadelphia, that state group came forth with the following resolution:

> The Republican Party is mindful of its obligations to the loyal women of America for their noble devotion to the cause of freedom; their admission to wider fields of usefulness is received with satisfaction; and the honest demands of any class of citizens for equal rights should be treated with respectful consideration.

Mrs. Stanton was skeptical; so was Susan, but she was willing to give the Philadelphia Republicans credit for a good effort, and she did some speaking on their behalf.

In the latter weeks of October Susan was in Rochester. She was a little worried about Guelma's poor health. Her older sister had known the grievous deaths of a daughter and an only son, and was not robust herself. Their mother, Lucy Anthony, was old and becoming frail. Only Mary was blooming. She had recently been made principal of the school where she had taught; she welcomed every visit of Susan's but unselfishly urged her not to stay home, but go on with her career.

On the second day of her visit a notice in the newspapers caught Susan's eye. It read:

> Now register! Today and tomorrow are the only remaining opportunities . . . on election day, less than a week hence, hundreds of you are likely to lose your votes

because you have not thought it worth while to give the five minutes. . . . Register now!

The paper dropped into Susan's lap. Of course, the notice was meant for men, but . . . ? Why not try?

Immediately she was on her feet, running upstairs for her bonnet, running downstairs to tell Guelma and then hurrying down the street to call upon certain, special people in Rochester—all of them women.

On November 1, the next day, sixteen ladies, most of them staid matrons, neatly and soberly dressed, walked to the registration office—which happened to be a shoemaker's shop on West Street—in a group. Susan entered first. The registration inspectors were startled and shocked, but they had had no instructions, and after a moment's hesitation they agreed she could register. Susan mentioned the Fourteenth Amendment, but it was the decent appearance of the ladies that influenced the inspectors.

One by one the ladies stepped up and signed their names: Miss Susan B. Anthony; Miss Mary S. Anthony; Mrs. Guelma McLean; Mrs. Hannah Mosher. Then came Mrs. Rhoda de Garmo, the Anthonys' old, dear friend from the days of the Underground Railway and the picnics on the farm. Then a Mrs. Sarah Truesdale; Mrs. Mary Pulver; Mrs. Mary S. Hebard; Mrs. Nancy M. Chapman; Mrs. Jane M. Coggswell; Mrs. Martha N. French; Mrs. Margaret Leyden; Mrs. Lottie Bolles Anthony; Mrs. Hannah Chatfield; Mrs. Susan M. Hough; Miss Ellen T. Baker.

Their registration caused only a ripple of amusement in Rochester, but on November 5 those same sixteen ladies went to the polls to vote, and that was a different story. Now the inspectors did try to stop them, but there were their names officially enrolled, officially accepted as citizens and voters, and there was nothing the angry, baffled gentlemen could do but let them cast their ballots.

The women's actions precipitated quite a commotion, and the shock waves traveled all over the country. Newspapers quoted the Fourteenth Amendment both for and against the women voting. The few who were in favor of the actions stuck with section one: "All persons born or naturalized in the United States . . . are citizens of the United States . . ."; while the majority, who were against, frantically culled from the other sections the words that would condemn what Susan and the fifteen others had done.

Part of the Fourteenth Amendment said: "Any person . . . who shall vote without having a legal right to vote; or do any unlawful act to secure . . . an opportunity to vote . . . shall be deemed guilty of a crime . . . and shall be punished by a fine not exceeding $500 or imprisonment not exceeding three years . . . or both at the discretion of the Court . . ."

The sixteen women well knew what they faced. Either they won by their action the constitutional right of all women to vote, or they might pay heavy fines and spend years in jail. They were afraid, but not one would back down.

Susan was accustomed to thinking and planning ahead, and now she went in search of a good lawyer to give her advice. She finally found one in the person of Henry R. Selden, formerly a judge in the Court of Appeals, and a highly respected, learned man.

He listened to her. "Come back on Monday morning, Miss Anthony, and let me think about this," he advised.

When she saw him after the weekend he was thoroughly on her side. "Section one of the Fourteenth Amendment gives you the right to vote," he said, "and I will be happy to act for you if the need arises."

The need did arise. On November 28, Thanksgiving Day, Mrs. Anthony opened her front door at a knock, and found chief marshal Keeney on the doorstep with warrants for the arrest of Susan, Mary and Guelma. The marshal was highly embarrassed. "The ladies," he mumbled, "may walk by themselves to the courthouse. I'll keep behind them and no one on the street will know what is happening."

"You will take me by force, marshal, or not at all," said Susan. "I want it known that I do not go willingly, that I do not accept the fact that my actions should lead to a court of justice."

So the poor chief marshal was forced to keep a hand upon her and another upon Mary, with Guelma under his eye, all the way along the streets, with people turning to stare and whisper.

The Anthony sisters were brought into the office of the commissioner of elections, where they found some of their co-defendants, and others, arriving. The commissioner, using psychology, tried to scare them and lower their morale by making them sit there for the whole day without speaking a word to them. Occasionally Susan would go up to the constable on duty at the door and demand that some official come and speak to them; he only shrugged. The door was locked.

It was evening before a key was heard in the lock, the door opened and the commissioner strolled in. "You will have to come back tomorrow, ladies. We've been waiting for the district attorney; he won't be here until tomorrow morning."

When Mrs. de Garmo protested at the treatment they had received, he snapped at her that she was a person under arrest; the warrant was still in effect; he was being generous in allowing her to go home instead of locking her up for the night.

The next morning the district attorney was there and he wasted no time. As soon as all the women were present he concentrated his questions upon Susan, and they all had to do with what had transpired between herself and Judge Selden. Susan quickly sensed that he was trying to establish that the Judge not only acted as her lawyer *after* she had voted, but had conspired beforehand to get her to vote.

When he saw he was getting nowhere with this line of questioning he declared a recess. Another hearing would be held that afternoon.

By afternoon the courthouse was besieged by Rochester women who had come out to protest the arrest and support the sixteen women. The commissioner had to move the hearing into a big room to accommodate the spectators, and the district attorney declared he had enough evidence for a trial.

Judge Selden shouldered his way through the crowd and sat beside Susan. The district attorney had hoped to eliminate him as lawyer for the defense by making him a co-criminal in a conspiracy, but he had failed. He had no more questions. The commissioner asked only enough to establish that it was indeed these sixteen who had registered on that certain day and place and who had voted, then he allowed the women only one or two words—"guilty" or "not guilty." They all said "not guilty." They were placed on bail of five hundred dollars each and ordered to appear for trial in Albany in January.

Within the next few weeks fifteen of the women were notified that it would not be necessary for them to appear in the Albany court. A test case would be made of Miss Susan B. Anthony only; the rest would not go to trial.

Nor would Susan go immediately into a trial court. She had to first face a grand jury, in January, which handed down the following solemn indictment that "Susan B. Anthony of Rochester had knowingly, wrongfully, and unlawfully voted (the said Susan B. Anthony being then and there a person of the female sex) contrary to the form of the statute and against the peace of the United States of America and their dignity." The grand jury bound Susan over to the marshall for custody and the actual trial would be in the Rochester court.

The poor marshal had never had such an obstreperous prisoner. She was out on bail, but she was supposed to remain in Rochester, under his eye. Susan would do no such thing. She had meetings to attend, speeches to make and an annual suffrage convention in Washington, D.C. to go to. The marshal went to the railroad station with her each time she left, protesting and pleading, but he never dared to stop her.

The convention was unusually well-attended. There were almost as many newspapermen there as delegates, and they scribbled furiously when Susan made the opening address.

"I stand here," she said, "under indictment for having exercised my right as a citizen to vote at the last election; and by a fiction of the law, I am now in custody and not a free person on this platform." She went on to tell why and how she had come to vote, interrupted by cheering from the delegates. The convention wholeheartedly stood behind her and the other women who had been arrested, and passed resolutions upholding the right of woman suffrage under existing laws.

The delegates went home to spread the word, and the newspapers of the country made headlines of it.

One newspaper and one editor made no mention of the event. Horace Greeley had died the past November. Whether he would have approved of Susan's action was doubtful, since he had approved of little she had done in the last few years.

Nevertheless, she and all the Anthonys mourned him. They remembered him for all his staunch support of the Abolitionists and that he had once been a firm advocate of woman's rights.

Another grief was coming even closer to the heart of the Anthony family. Guelma was truly ill. She had forced herself to go and register and then vote and had appeared at the hearings, but it was a very sick woman who had nerved herself to do these things. Her lungs were seriously affected; she lost weight until she was only a pitiful skeleton of her former pretty self.

No matter how worried Susan was for her, she had to go out and lecture. She had to raise the fees for her lawyer and for court costs; the suffrage convention had not been able to vote a penny for her. Susan went from lecture to lecture, with only half her mind on what she was saying. Her tension over Guelma was so great Susan fainted in the middle of one speech.

Because of her ill health, the Court discharged Mrs. Guelma McLean entirely from the case.

Since the trial was not scheduled until May 13, Susan was able to go to the New York suffrage convention which celebrated the twenty-fifth anniversay of the first convention in Seneca Falls. The celebration was to feature the two founders of Seneca Falls: Mrs. Stanton and Lucretia Mott. Neither one of these great women minded in the least that two other people stole the show from them! One was Susan B. Anthony, cheered as she began her speech by saying she stood there a prisoner.

The other? The door of the stage opened quietly while Susan was speaking and an unforgettable, huge, dark man whose grizzled hair was touched with grey, walked in. Susan

turned and stretched out her hands. "Frederick Douglass!"
Then there was a tumult of rejoicing all over the hall.

Their great friend, one of the first to champion woman's
rights, was back with them. Even though he was much too
busy working with Southern Black leaders trying to forge a
real reconstruction of the South to give any time to the
women's movement, he was with them in spirit.

Susan returned to Rochester to find that the district attorney had got a postponement of the trial and was demanding
it be changed to another county. Miss Anthony, he claimed,
had been touring all around Rochester and Monroe County
and stirring up sympathy. For a fair trial he insisted it be held
in the town of Canandaigua, Ontario County. The judge
agreed, setting June 17 as the opening of the trial.

Susan had one month. She sent out a call to women speakers to come and help explain the case to the people of Ontario
County, in the hope of combatting prejudice and getting a
jury which would be disposed to listen to her case and try it
fairly.

Only one woman responded. Matilda Joslyn Gage was a new
recruit to the woman suffrage movement. She had never
spoken in public but she had a brilliant mind. Her defense of
Susan's actions had all the logic of the best of legal brains.
Without any education as a lawyer or speaker, she was naturally good at both.

Chapter Nine

On the morning of June 17, 1873, Susan Brownell Anthony, dressed in dark silk and a white lace collar borrowed from Mary, walked up the steps of the Canandaigua courthouse. On one side of her marched the distinguished figure of her lawyer, the former Judge Selden; on the other was her sister, Hannah. The bells were tolling for the opening of court, and people were flocking from all over.

Lawyers were there in their best broadcloth, but there were also, thronging and pushing around Susan, the usual idlers who attended court as they would any show; the same idlers who sat and whittled on the courthouse steps in good weather or sat and gossiped around the stoves of country stores in winter.

They snickered and pointed at her; they crowded around to get a good look at her; they made remarks.

If they thought to embarrass her they were disappointed. A woman who had had rotten eggs thrown at her wasn't bothered by stupid insults. Susan only regretted that the other fifteen women-voters were not there that day.

The trial had been postponed so many times; the women had shown up so many times only to be told to go home, that they had not believed this was the real thing.

It was. The trial was to begin which would decide whether a woman was a citizen or a subject of the United States.

Susan entered the courtroom and sat at the table of the defense lawyer, while Hannah took a seat in the front row bench. In no time the benches were all full and men were standing at the back; courtroom attendants were turning people away.

The United States District Attorney, the Honorable Richard Crowley, prosecuting, took his place at the table opposite, placing papers and notebooks and pens in front of him. Then the clerk rapped with a gavel and everyone stood up as His Honor, Judge Ward Hunt, came in and took his presiding seat at the high bench. He nodded.

He spoke, and the trial could proceed. "In the United States Circuit Court, Northern District of New York . . ." droned the clerk, ". . . case of the United States of America versus Susan B. Anthony. The Honorable Ward Hunt, Presiding . . . for the United States appearing the Honorable Richard Crowley; for the defendant, the Honorable Henry R. Selden and John Van Voorhis, Esquire."

"Is Mr. Crowley in court?"

"Here, Your Honor."

"Is Mr. Selden and his associate here for the defense?"

"Here, Your Honor."

As Judge Selden sat down again he leaned over and whispered to Susan: "Bad luck. I thought we were supposed to get Judge Hall. Hunt will do whatever Washington tells him to." He looked at the audience over Susan's shoulder. "You should be flattered, Miss Anthony, at the crowd you are getting. Millard Fillmore just came in."

"The former president?"

"The same."

SUSAN B. ANTHONY

The morning passed in the tedious job of selecting the jury of twelve men who would try the case. Lunch intervened and it was 2:30 before the last man was chosen and the trial could get down to business.

Mr. Crowley, for the plaintiff, the United States of America, opened with a short speech:

May it please the Court and the Gentlemen of the Jury: On the 5th of November, 1872, there was held . . . a general election for different officers, and among those, for candidates in the Congress of the United States. The defendant, Miss Susan B. Anthony, at that time resided in the city of Rochester . . . and upon the 5th day of November, 1872, she voted for a representative in the Congress of the United States, to represent the 29th District of this State . . . in the Congress of the United States. At that time she was a woman.

He paused. Some in the audience snickered. Some of the jurymen smiled. But Mr. Crowley frowned, as if to say that while there might be reason for the snickers, this was after all a court of law and a crime had been committed.

"I suppose," he continued, "that there is no question about that. The question in this case . . . will be rather a question of law than of fact."

As he went on Susan knew that she and Henry Selden were in agreement with the prosecutor on that point. She was not going to deny that she was a woman and had voted; what was before the Court and jury was the validity of her vote.

The Honorable Mr. Crowley pointed out to the jury that he was speaking on behalf of the government when he declared that Miss Anthony had unlawfully cast her ballot. Even if she *thought* she had a right, it did not make her action any less a crime. She had violated the law. He read statutes and rulings and part of the Fourteenth Amendment to the jury, to back up his claim. With his opening statement concluded, Mr. Crowley sat down.

Before the prosecution could begin its case by calling its witnesses, Henry Selden was on his feet. The judge recognized him, giving him permission to speak.

"Your Honor, Gentlemen of the Jury, the defense wishes to concede that Miss Susan B. Anthony is indeed a woman," said Mr. Selden, making a slight gesture with his hand towards Susan, seated at his right. His gesture had the effect of directing all eyes to her, and she met them with serene composure and quiet dignity.

This time there were no snickers and no smiles. Something about the woman in the simple dress and the white lace collar, with her plain, honest, decent face and her quiet, intelligent eyes, changed almost everyone's attitude to respect. Guilty she might be and rash, but there was that strong, down-to-earth quality about her that made the men on the jury study her with fresh interest.

This was a small town and a farming community. The way Susan looked, the way her clasped hands showed the signs of physical toil, made them think of women of their own families.

Mr. Crowley very quickly put the Rochester inspector of elections on the witness stand, and the examination began to establish the absolute facts of just how, where and when the crime was committed.

This was routine. Susan took this chance to study the prosecutor, the judge and the jury. Mr. Crowley was fashionably attired in a black suit; he had the fashionable, impressive manners of a big-time state lawyer. Judge Ward Hunt was not so impressive. True, he was also dressed in a fine black suit, but the face above it was—as she later described him—"pale-faced, prim-looking," and he looked like a man of few brains and a large conceit.

She pinned what hopes she had on her lawyer, her own chance on the witness stand and the jury.

Thus it was a great shock to her and Selden when the judge absolutely refused to allow Susan to take the witness stand in her own defense when it came time for the prosecution to rest its case and the defense to begin questioning.

Selden raged, coming as close to contempt as he could without being removed from the courtroom. Why should not the defendant be allowed to speak in her own behalf, as was the right of all defendants? The district attorney declared she was not competent to testify; the judge upheld him. When Selden persisted, he was told the Court's ruling on that was final.

There was only one thing to do then, and Selden did it magnificently. The judge could not prevent him, as a lawyer, from speaking in Miss Anthony's behalf, and Henry Selden spoke for three hours, telling the jury everything Susan would have said: that women had never been excluded in the Constitution from citizenship, that until the recent amendments there had been no distinction of "male" or "female" and that Susan B. Anthony had as much right to vote under the wording of most of the Constitution as any man.

The United States attorney was on his feet frequently, objecting that this was not relevant. The judge tried his best to check Mr. Selden, but the defense lawyer was within his rights to speak, and speak he did.

At last the judge interrupted. Court was hastily adjourned for the day.

The next morning Susan was pleased to see that five of the Rochester women who had voted with her had come to the trial, and that there were other women in the courtroom audience.

Henry Selden had not finished his defense. He stood before the judge and the jury and put forth his legal position, that the case boiled down to three propositions, two of which were matters of law and must be decided by the judge, and one of fact which must be decided by the jury. The first was that the defendant had a lawful right to vote; the second, that whether she had a lawful right to vote or not, if she honestly believed that she had that right and voted in good faith in that belief, she was guilty of no crime; third, that when she gave her vote she gave it in good faith, believing that it was her right to do so.

The first point, Selden and Susan believed, the judge would undoubtedly rule against, but on the second point it seemed to them he had to acknowledge that Susan thought she had the right. The last point, which the jury would decide, would declare her guilty or innocent, and Selden thought there was a better than even chance they would let her go free.

Mr. Crowley now argued on the first two points. With almost indecent haste, as if he had already rehearsed it, Judge Hunt gave his decision.

The defendant did *not* have a lawful right to vote. Whether she honestly believed she had that right or not constituted no defense. She was bound to know she was not a legal voter, and even if she voted in good faith in the contrary belief, "it constituted no defense to the crime with which she was charged."

Then Judge Hunt shocked the entire courtroom (except

147

for Mr. Crowley, who looked smug) by announcing that his decision on those two points disposed of the whole case and left no question of fact for the jury. He turned to the jury and directed them to find a verdict of guilty.

Henry Selden had leaped to his feet. "That is a direction no Court has power to make in a criminal case!"

The judge tried to ignore him and speak to the clerk, but Selden—who had been a judge himself and knew his law—demanded that the case be submitted to the jury and that the judge must instruct the jury that "if the defendant, at the time of voting, believed she had a right to vote, and voted in good faith . . . she is not guilty of the offense charged . . ."

Judge Hunt rapped and rapped with his gavel and, taking advantage of a pause in Selden's objections, said quickly to the clerk:

"Take the verdict, Mr. Clerk."

The clerk then said: "Gentlemen of the jury, hearken to your verdict as the Court has recorded it. You say you find the defendant guilty of the offense whereof she stands indicted, and so say you all."

The jury, of course, had said nothing of the kind. They sat stunned and bewildered and confused. What was going on?

The outraged Selden would not give up. "Will the clerk poll the jury?" He was within his rights to ask that each juryman be individually asked if that was, indeed, his verdict.

"No," said the judge. He turned to the jury and told them: "Gentlemen of the jury, you are discharged."

The twelve men, obedient to the judge and to the dismissing wave of the clerk's hand, filed out of the jury box and out of the courtroom. The judge rose. Court was dismissed for the day.

As soon as he was gone bedlam broke out. Visiting lawyers and other judges either crowded around Selden or tried their best to avoid him; newspapermen hurried between Selden and Crowley for statements. The judge's action was unheard-of. Whether the newspapermen or the lawyers cared anything for woman's rights or Miss Anthony's beliefs, she was a defendant in a criminal trial and entitled to a trial by jury. If Judge Hunt's decision was to set a precedent it could destroy one of America's most cherished legal protections. A judge could simply tell a jury that he had decided and they had voted, when they had not done any such thing!

Henry Selden and his young assistant, John Van Voorhis, spoke freely to the newspapermen of their shock and disgust that such a mockery of justice had taken place that day, but when they were alone with Susan they discussed it quietly. Judge Hunt, both realized, did not have the brains to plan such a maneuver; his instructions had come from more ruthless men, men in government who had correctly seen that this was no small trial in an obscure court in a little town— rather, it was of national importance.

Under no circumstances was the judge to risk a possible favorable jury decision, swayed by Selden or Susan.

John Van Voorhis was to say, later: "If Miss Anthony had won her case on the merits, it would have revolutionized the suffrage of the country and enfranchised every woman in the United States."

The next day the court reconvened for sentencing. And Judge Hunt made his one mistake. He asked the usual and correct question: "Has the prisoner anything to say why sentence should not be pronounced?"

Susan certainly did.

Judge Hunt must have forgotten that Susan B. Anthony made her living by making speeches. She rose from her chair as confidently as if she were on her usual platform, and launched into a full lecture on woman's rights. Henry Selden leaned back, delighted. Even if she had lost the case, she was getting her day in court, and every word she said was being heard by newspapermen and going into the official court record.

"Yes, Your Honor, I have many things to say," Susan began, "for in your ordered verdict of guilty, you have trampled under foot every vital principle of our government. My natural rights, my civil rights, my political rights, my judicial rights, are all alike ignored. Robbed of the fundamental privilege of citizenship, I am degraded from the status of a citizen to that of a subject; and not only myself individually . . ."

The judge was now aghast at the storm he had loosed upon his own head. He interrupted. "The Court cannot listen to a rehearsal of arguments the prisoner's counsel has already consumed three hours in presenting."

Serenely the defendant went on speaking: "May it please Your Honor, I am not arguing the question, but simply stating the reasons why sentence cannot, in justice, be pronounced against me. Your denial of my citizen's right to vote is the denial of my right of consent as one of the governed, the denial of my right of representation as one of the taxed, the denial of my right to a trial by a jury of my peers . . ."

Someone in the audience whispered loudly: "What a lawyer she would have made!"

The judge leaned over his high desk. "The Court cannot allow the prisoner to go on!"

Susan replied: "But Your Honor will not deny me this one and only poor privilege of protest against this high-handed outrage upon my citizen's rights." And she started right back to the November 5 day when she had walked in to vote and started to say why . . .

Judge Hunt shouted: "The prisoner must sit down—the Court cannot allow it . . . !"

He did not know how many years Susan had handled hecklers and bullies who had tried to stop her from speaking. Her voice simply overrode the judge's and she went right on with what she wanted to say, which was a marvelous legal exposition of the status of women under American law. A prisoner in a trial such as this was entitled by law to a trial by her "peers," her equals. But since the judge had ruled she was not a citizen then she had no peers in that courtroom. All—the prosecutor, the judge and the jury—were men; therefore, they were her superiors. She was merely a subject, and that was how she had been treated.

Doubtless Selden had put this legal thought into her head, but Susan was speaking extemporaneously, without any notes, and marshaling her points into superb logic that impressed everyone and nearly drove the judge frantic. He yelled:

"The Court must insist—the prisoner has been tried according to the established forms of law." He found himself on the defensive before Susan's attack.

". . . by forms of law all made by men, interpreted by men, administered by men, in favor of men and against women," Susan rebuked the judge, as if she had the authority to lecture him, as she certainly thought she did. "And hence, Your Honor's *ordered* verdict of guilty, against a United States citizen for the exercise of 'that citizen's right to vote,' simply because that citizen was a woman and not a man." She went on to remind him, sternly, that in that very courtroom men had been sentenced for befriending runaway slaves. Now there were no more slaves; the law had been proved wrong. So it would be in the future, when women had their right to a voice in the government. The slaves, under the unjust law, took their freedom in their own hands and defied the law—"and I have taken mine, and mean to take it at every opportunity."

Judge Hunt was red-faced with rage. "The Court orders the prisoner to sit down."

She would sit when she was ready. She finished what she had to say and then turned to Mr. Selden, who stood up and pulled back the chair for her, as if this plain woman were a queen.

Judge Hunt, unprepared, had just started to tell her to sit down; he had to reverse himself in midair and tell her to stand up for sentencing. Susan did. Judge Hunt wasted not a second, he was so afraid she might start talking again. He blurted out:

"The sentence of the Court is that you pay a fine of one hundred dollars and the costs of the prosecution."

He gathered up his papers and rose, which was the usual signal for all to rise and adjourn, but the prisoner was not finished with him.

"May it please Your Honor, I shall never pay a dollar of your unjust penalty. . . . and I shall earnestly and persistently continue to urge all women to the practical recognition of the old revolutionary maxim, that 'Resistance to tyranny is obedience to God.' "

The judge fled. Susan B. Anthony had had the final word.

In one way Selden rejoiced at the light sentence, knowing as he did that she had no money to fight any appeals. Yet his lawyer's sense was outraged that whoever was prompting Judge Hunt behind the scenes had been clever enough *not* to include in the sentence that Susan must stay in prison until the fine was paid. This was the usual procedure. If this had happened Henry Selden would have had to take the appeal up to the Supreme Court because the judge had refused his client a real jury trial.

As it was, since the Court never made the slightest effort to collect the hundred dollar fine or the costs of the prosecution, Selden had too weak a case to appeal—especially in the face of the prejudice against women he was certain to encounter.

The newspaper stories all over the United States brought Susan a flood of letters from sympathizers, and many of the messages also included small checks—so many they finally amounted to more than a thousand dollars. Not one penny of this money did she spend to ease her own personal debt from the *Revolution*.

Two hundred and fifteen dollars went to Selden and Van Voorhis; they refused to take any more from her. Instead, Judge Selden suggested that the three of them prepare a full report of the trial, getting as much as possible from the Court record, have it printed and put in pamphlet form and distribute it as widely as possible. The suggestion was excellent. The pamphlets were well-received and passed on from hand to hand, from city to city.

In addition to these expenses Susan had another. The three inspectors who had allowed her to register and vote had also been arrested. When Susan and the fifteen other women had gone to register, the inspectors had warned her they might get into trouble. Susan declared herself willing to pay any fine they incurred, and so they had gone ahead and let the women register.

Now they had had their trial and each was fined twenty-five dollars. Susan asked them to refuse to pay, on principle, and they were gallant enough to agree, but eventually she had to pay to save them from going to jail.

The trial of the inspectors had gone on without her being able to attend it. Guelma had collapsed and Susan was the only member of the family free to nurse her. Their mother was over eighty and frail; Hannah had her own household to care for, although she took over from Susan whenever she could; Mary was teaching school. For four long months Susan poured her own strength into trying to keep her beloved older sister alive, but Guelma died on November 9, 1873.

It was fortunate for Susan, numbed with sorrow, that she was forced to get out of the house and resume lecturing to pay off that old newspaper debt. Some of her debtors felt they had been patient long enough and were pressing her, although a few were more than generous.

Shortly after Guelma's death a Quaker cousin of Susan's, Anson Lapham, invited her to his home for Thanksgiving dinner, and there he gave her back all the notes she had signed when she had borrowed money from him years ago to keep the *Revolution* going. The canceled notes amounted to four thousand dollars and was a big chunk out of the original ten thousand.

There was still a lot left to pay, however. Most of her lectures earned only thirty dollars each, and her transportation and expenses had to come out of that. Already three years had passed trying to get out from under debt and there were more years to come.

Susan did find that her audiences were growing. She was the heroine—or the criminal, depending upon the viewpoint —of a trial. She also wrote a whole new lecture called "Bread and the Ballot"—about work and wages for women—and found it to be immensely popular. She was well on her way to the end of her financial problems when Hannah suddenly fell ill of the same lung trouble as Guelma.

It was known that Colorado and California claimed cures for this illness. The Anthony family reasoned that Kansas would be just as good, not realizing that it was the high dryness that was best. Hannah was rushed to Daniel's home in Leavenworth, and Susan sent her six hundred dollars.

In this terrible situation, as all the Moshers moved to be close to Hannah, and as Susan worked steadily to help them financially, they were all grateful for one thing. The very elderly Mrs. Anthony could not take this new disaster, and she gently and painlessly slipped into a twilight world of mental blankness. She was childlike and happy, with her daughter Mary, her son-in-law Aaron and a succession of young lady teacher lodgers, all living in her house.

Even though Susan knew Hannah was dying there was one task, in addition to earning money for her, that she had to do. She had to go to the Philadelphia Centennial.

Eighteen seventy-six—one hundred years from the founding of a new nation—the United States had something special to celebrate in Philadelphia: the fact they were still united. Enough time had passed since the end of the Civil War that white Southerners and Northerners could meet and mingle without bitterness.

The official proceedings—speeches and statements—would go into a record which would be set aside for a future America to read, during the next Centennial in 1976. All sorts of special interests wanted to have something to say in that record. There would be much said about the progress of the Blacks in the South, hiding the truth of the white man's whip. There would be every attempt made to have the official Centennial record show nothing but sweetness and light.

SUSAN B. ANTHONY

The National Woman Suffrage Association was determined that American women in the future would know that
American women in 1876 were fighting injustice. They
laid their plans well, organized their attack movements and
chose the soldiers who would go in and brave the enemy.

Lucretia Mott declared herself too old for an active part,
and so did Elizabeth Cady Stanton, now nearly sixty and
getting fat. These women would help plot strategy behind the
scenes, but Susan B. Anthony and Mrs. Matilda Gage would
make the actual move. Susan was only six years younger
than Mrs. Stanton but, somehow, she was always considered
one of the "younger" ones.

The acting vice-president of the United States, Senator
Ferry, was to preside at the official ceremonies. Only people
holding special tickets would be allowed seats inside Independence Hall; the general public would crowd the park
outside. Susan managed to get herself and four other women
tickets as representatives of the Leavenworth *Times*, her
brother's paper.

On July 4 the five women were among the first to be admitted to the hall, thus getting their choice of seats down
in the first rows. They had a long wait and it was blisteringly
hot; people on all sides were fanning themselves and opening collars and ties; the five women sat quietly and still,
except that the other four constantly cast side glances at
Susan. She was to give them the signal.

One after another statesman and politician came forth on
the platform to orate, but finally came the awesome moment
of the reading of the Declaration of Independence. Susan
had said beforehand this would most likely be the appropri-
ate moment for them to act. All five women tensed themselves.

Luck came to their aid. No sooner was the Declaration

read than the brass band began to play the Brazilian national anthem in honor of the Brazilian emperor, a leading guest of honor. Everyone rose. Susan gave her signal. Since everyone was standing and shuffling his feet and stretching his muscles, it was not immediately noticed that Susan and the other four women had sidled out of their places and walked to the front, until they stood directly in front of the vice-president.

Susan spoke to him. Automatically he put out his hand and she placed in it what was the women's own declaration, or rather, their impeachment of the government. Mr. Ferry had for a long time been friendly to woman suffrage. Another man might have handed the paper back or even thrown it away. He took it, bowed and kept it in his hand.

Then the five women turned and faced the audience. By now everyone knew something exciting had taken place. The five slowly walked back up the aisle and as they did so handed out, right and left, dozens and dozens of the same statement they had given Mr. Ferry.

Outside, word of their bold and daring act had preceded them. The crowd was bored with just milling around and having nothing to do; Susan and Mrs. Gage quickly saw their chance. They hurried to the empty bandstand, climbed onto it, and the crowd gathered around it, growing in numbers every moment. Then Susan read aloud the Declaration of Woman's Rights.

It was a long recital of the injustices done to women and it ended: "We ask of our rulers at this hour no special favors, no special privileges, no special legislation. We ask justice, we ask equality, we ask that all the civil and political rights that belong to citizens of the United States be guaranteed to us and our daughters forever."

The crowd was wakened out of its heat-sodden torpor.

SUSAN B. ANTHONY

They cheered and jeered. They talked among themselves and argued. The newspapermen had raced out of Independence Hall and were surrounding the women. This was news.

And the newspapermen, along with quite a few of the spectators, followed the five women to the Unitarian Church where Lucretia Mott and Mrs. Stanton were already warming up a big audience. Mrs. Gage reported the successful battle maneuver. One of the liveliest and most interesting meetings followed, with one good speaker after another.

What pleased Susan most were the new young leaders: Belva Lockwood, who would be the first woman lawyer admitted to argue cases before the Supreme Court; Esther Morris, justice of the peace in Wyoming; Lillie Devereux Blake; Phoebe Couzins; and Mrs. Gage. While each one spoke, Susan listened with an ear for those who could and would carry on the work.

Not that she meant to quit just yet. She still had her health and strength and was still in demand to lecture. But the terrific drive for constant lecturing was gone. Her debt had at last been paid. On May 1, just before she had come to join Mrs. Stanton to make plans for the Centennial, she had paid the last dollar of the money she had long ago borrowed for the *Revolution.*

So it was a Susan free of personal worries who picked up the newspapers the day after the Centennial ceremonies and read "SCANDAL AT INDEPENDENCE HALL—WOMEN INVADE HISTORIC CELEBRATION—DEMAND VOTE —SUFFRAGISTS INSULT GOVERNMENT . . ."

Good, Susan thought. If only a few more women would come forth and do more insulting they might get places. Susan was no fanatic feminist; she did not blame men for everything. She was equally disgusted with those women who liked being considered "dear, silly, little things" and having doors opened for them by gallants, and being treated like dolls instead of human beings.

Oh, if she could only have an army of women who would rather be men's partners than their puppets! Let them come in silks and ribbons and perfume, or in calico and patches— but let them come!

Chapter Ten

In May, 1877, Hannah died, and three years later Susan's mother quietly passed away. Her will left her house to Mary, which was a wise move on the part of Lucy Anthony, since she knew that Susan would very likely have mortgaged and lost it for her cause. Now Susan was assured of a home with Mary for her old age.

She was by no means old at sixty, and she had a new project. Now that Mrs. Stanton had definitely retired from going out on lecture tours, the two women began the monumental task of writing a history of woman suffrage. Mrs. Stanton was the more fluent and would do most of the actual writing, but it was Susan who had the job of gathering and organizing all the material they—and others—had collected for more than twenty-five years.

Susan and Mrs. Stanton sat facing each other across the desk at the Stanton home. Beside them were piles of newspaper clippings, old placards, pamphlets, advertisements, notices of meetings, speeches, letters and telegrams. These all had to be put in order by dates and places and persons. Then Susan traveled to the homes of elderly ladies and ransacked their cupboards for more records; she came back with trunks of information.

The Stantons moved to Tenafly and the history project

had a room to itself, called the Tower, where Susan prodded Mrs. Stanton to work.

They wrote honestly. Although they were frequently disgusted with the polite approach of the American Woman's Suffrage Association, they gave the leaders full credit for their part in the history of the struggle for women's rights. Such figures as Lucy Stone, William Lloyd Garrison, Mary Livermore and Julia Ward Howe received their full due as Mrs. Stanton's pen scratched along the reams and reams of paper.

She was fairer than they. When Garrison wrote his own story of the antislavery struggle, he very pointedly omitted Susan B. Anthony's name from it. That was shocking. He well knew all she had done.

The American Woman's Suffrage Association thought it very nice of Susan and Elizabeth to write this history. It was a ladylike and cultured thing to do, instead of getting oneself arrested for voting or pushing one's way into the formal Independence Day proceedings. The *Women's Journal* refused to even discuss a Sixteenth Amendment, but it spoke kindly of the forthcoming history.

Wendell Phillips, especially, thought that perhaps he had been a little too hasty in his judgment of Susan. In spite of himself, he was coming to have a higher opinion of her than he had before. He couldn't help but admire such courage and persistence; the way she held straight to the mark.

While Susan was working with Mrs. Stanton on the second volume of the history that winter, a letter came to her from Phillips.

"Dear Susan," he wrote . . .

Dear Susan! she thought. Whatever had come over the man?

She started again.

SUSAN B. ANTHONY

Dear Susan: Our friend, Mrs. Eddy, Francis Jackson's daughter, died a week ago Thursday. At her request, I made her will some weeks before. Her man of business, Mr. C. R. Ransom, is the executor. He and I were present and consulted, and we know all her intentions and wishes from long talks with her in years gone by. After making various bequests, she ordered the remainder divided equally between you and Lucy Stone. There is no question whatever that your portion will be $25,000 or $28,000. I advised her, in order to avoid all lawyers, to give this sum to you outright, with no responsibility to any one or any court, only 'requesting you to use it for the advancement of the Woman's Rights cause.' . . . Faithfully yours, Wendell Phillips.

There was a mist before Susan's eyes as she folded and refolded the letter, and she had to take off her glasses—which she had started using—and polish them briskly. She swallowed. She *would* not cry.

"What is it, Susan?" asked Mrs. Stanton.

Susan handed over the letter. She could only say, gruffly, "About time," but in her heart was a welling of gratitude to her old-time friend. She knew very well that Wendell Phillips could have persuaded Mrs. Eddy to leave all the money to Lucy Stone. He hadn't. He had thought of her.

Susan answered his letter in a way to heal the breach between them. "How worthy the daughter of Francis Jackson! How little thought have I had all these years that she cherished this marvellous trust in me, and now I recognize in her munificent legacy your own faith in me. . . . So to you, my dear friend, as to her, my unspeakable gratitude goes out. May I prove worthy. . . ."

SUSAN B. ANTHONY

It took three years before the money was finally given to
Susan, three years in which Wendell Phillips did his best for
her, fighting against a suit brought by a relation of the dead
woman to break the will. The will stood. In 1885 Susan
would have more than twenty thousand dollars to promote
the cause.

Before that happened Mrs. Stanton was in England and
urged Susan to come. Elizabeth Cady wanted a vacation before finishing the third volume of the history. Susan scoffed.
All very well for Mrs. Stanton who needed such things as
vacations, and whose oldest daughter was in London and
oldest son in Paris, but why should she go? Besides, she
couldn't afford it.

A new, young, ardent (and wealthy) suffragist, Rachel
Foster, concocted a plan. A European tour was the proper
way to round out a wealthy American girl's education, but
Rachel couldn't go unless she had a chaperon. Couldn't Miss
Anthony accompany her, all expenses paid? And thus give
herself a chance to see how the woman's rights movement
was doing in other countries?

It was an offer Susan couldn't refuse.

They sailed in February, 1883, and did not return until
November, right after Mrs. Stanton's daughter, Harriet, had
given birth to the first grandchild. During those months
young Rachel was hard put to keep up with her chaperon.
Susan's energy wore her out. They saw every "sight" in Italy,
Switzerland and France; they visited leading suffrage figures
in those countries, but it was Great Britain most of all that
thrilled Susan.

There the suffragists were as alive, as eager and bold, as she
was. She met Dr. and Emmeline Pankhurst and was impressed by both. However, the suffrage movement in England

SUSAN B. ANTHONY

at that time was split into a lot of small groups, unable to unite, and this seemed to put an end to a great new idea of Susan's. She had wanted to build an international woman's rights movement.

On the very last evening before the boat sailed, she and Mrs. Stanton were given a farewell banquet. When it came for Susan to answer the flowery compliments she astounded them all by proposing that, then and there, they constitute themselves an international committee to help each other in any way they could. It was so decided.

A seed had been planted which would grow beyond Susan's dreams.

The next February Wendell Phillips died; that April Susan met Lucy Stone for the first time in many years, as the two came together in the Boston lawyer's office to collect their legacies. They amounted to $24,125 each, of the Eddy money, and Susan took her share in bonds and stocks and securities and sewed them into her petticoat.

That night on the train she could not sleep for fear her wealth would be stolen, and she had time to think back to those years when both Phillips and Lucy Stone had been her models and guides. How glad she was that she and Wendell had renewed their friendship before his death, and how she wished that the breach with Lucy could be healed and the suffrage movement become one.

That wish came true four years later.

During that time she and Mrs. Stanton finished the third and final volume of the history, and had the great pleasure of seeing it well reviewed by newspapers and magazines. Editors called it a most important contribution to the history of the United States. The authors had rescued from oblivion the work of hundreds of men and women on behalf of suffrage.

164

Also during those years Susan continued to cross and re-cross the continent on speaking tours. Wherever she went she made converts. This was a great joy. It moved her to rejoicing to see new, young, intelligent girls coming forward to organize in their own communities. Even older women wrote her they had changed their minds after they heard her speak. She turned out to be not the ugly, shrewish spinster they had read about, who hated men because she had never had the chance to marry.

For so many years newspapers had written of her like this, and had drawn cruel caricatures of a hard-featured, bony creature striking out with a stick at all men, and at politicians in particular. But this was changing. Slowly the contempt was giving way to respect, and even to affection.

Susan couldn't understand it. She looked just the same. She had bought a garnet-colored velvet dress in London, but she kept it for special times, and still wore her plain silks. What she did not realize was how well they suited her. Tall and still slender, but broad-shouldered, with her plain healthy face and her hair parted in the center as she had always worn it, Susan B. Anthony at sixty-five had something better than beauty. She had distinction, poise and an effortless, unself-conscious way of being the center of attention wherever she was.

It was frequently necessary for Susan to be in Washington to confer with those congressmen favorable to her cause and to convince those who were wavering. She stayed in wealthy homes when she was there, with no false pride at accepting their charity. They weren't feeding *her*. They were donating to the cause.

As a result of all her experiences, the simple Quaker farm girl had acquired a knowledge of the world, and she was at home in any circle. Some things about her, though, never changed. She was blunt in her speech; said what she thought in simple words; never pretended; never put on airs.

Her friends and her correspondence grew. At one and the same time she was writing to England about an international meeting; writing to Oregon to help Miss Duniway in the struggle to get the state franchise for women; writing always to Mrs. Stanton; making a flying visit to Rochester to see Mary, who had retired from teaching and was looking after their two nieces; lobbying in Washington. Her best friend there was Senator Blair of Maine, whom she kept after constantly to get the woman's suffrage amendment before Congress.

He teased her. Instead of bothering him, he wrote her, "I wish you would go home and get married."

She could now take teasing, because she was finding out the deep affection behind it. To her amazement she was finding out that people could, and did, love her.

In 1887 Susan and Mrs. Stanton, because of their correspondence with suffragists abroad, could tell the time was ripe for an international meeting. They began to work. Susan, the organizer, did most of the inviting and arranging. Their National Woman Suffrage Association was to play hostess to women from other countries, particularly from Great Britain. They issued a call.

The call went out, not only to women abroad, but to women and organizations in America, and to Susan's great joy, the Boston group—the American Woman Suffrage Association—responded. They would come and among their delegates would be Lucy Stone Blackwell and Antoinette Brown.

Susan wrote immediately to Antoinette: "So, my dear, I am very, very glad that you and Lucy are both to be on our platform, and we are to stand together again after these twenty years. But none of the past!"

She was ready to forget and forge a new future for the American groups.

For the International Council Susan had booked the big opera house of Albaugh's in Washington, and it was packed. For eight solid days and nights there were speakers and introductions of women from forty-nine foreign nations and from organizations from every state of the United States. Foreign flags decorated the inside and outside; foreign correspondents were on hand to report the story for their own newspapers.

Elizabeth Cady Stanton gave the opening address. Lucy Stone was on the platform. Delegates spoke. And a new permanent International Council was formed, with Frances Willard elected as president of the branch that would be the American National Council.

Susan had picked her. Susan, busy planning and organizing, was everywhere. Delegates and newspapermen found it was easy to find her when they wanted her for a statement or for advice, because she was wearing a red silk shawl a friend had given her. It wasn't anything special. Susan only wore it because it was comfortable and warm. But everyone could pick out that spot of red in the crowd, and everyone knew enough to head for the shawl if they had a question.

The shawl was so comfortable she began to wear it to all her meetings. It became her badge. Several years later at a convention she showed up without it. There was a disturbance in the newspapermen's section and a note was handed up to her on the platform: "No red shawl, no report." She broke up in laughter, but she had to send to her hotel room for her shawl.

Both the American Suffrage Association and the National Suffrage Association wanted an end to their separation. They wanted unity. So did Susan and Lucy Stone. They differed sometimes in how suffrage was to be accomplished, but they both wanted the same ends. They were both honorable women. Susan was spending much of her share of the legacy to promote the history and pay for International Council meetings, while Lucy Stone was just as unselfishly spending hers on the *Woman's Journal*.

It took time and delicate negotiations but, finally, on January 21, 1889, an agreement was signed between the two organizations. Elections followed. Mrs. Stanton was chosen president; Susan B. Anthony was vice-president-at-large; Lucy Stone, chairman of the executive committee; Rachel Avery and Alice Stone Blackwell were secretaries.

It was a good compromise, since the National group was far larger and more powerful than the Boston group. And Mrs. Stanton left immediately for England on a trip, putting Susan in charge—which pleased the majority of the voters, who had voted for Elizabeth Cady since Susan had urged them to.

Out of this union, as Susan had hoped, came forth new leaders, and Susan kept them under her eye, always looking for the one or ones who would most surely carry on her work. There was the gifted lecturer, Anna Howard Shaw; there was Carrie Chapman Catt; Frances Willard; and others.

Susan B. Anthony was seventy years old in 1890. The great dining room of the Riggs Hotel in Washington was reserved for this event, and famous women from all over America gathered to do her honor. Old and young, they called her "Susan." They told her how well she looked, and she grinned at them, since she was wearing the same garnet velvet dress she had bought years ago in England. They spoke of a vacation for her, and the tall, straight-backed, white-haired woman looked at them owlishly over her spectacles and laughed.

The one moment when she came close to tears was when Mrs. Stanton rose to speak on "The Friendships of Women."

"Ours," she said, "has been a friendship of hard work and self-denial . . . Emerson says, 'It is better to be a thorn in the side of your friend than his echo.' If this adds weight and stability to friendship, then ours will endure forever, for we have indeed been thorns in the side of each other . . ."

Susan nodded. How many times had she had to drive Elizabeth Cady Stanton to work on a speech? How many times had Mrs. Stanton tried to sway Susan from financial follies, from throwing money into suffrage causes and going into debt?

"Dear friends," continued Mrs. Stanton, looking with love at Susan,

I have had no peace for forty years, since the day we started together on the suffrage expedition in search of woman's place in the . . . Constitution. . . . I sailed some years ago for England. With an ocean between us, I said, now I shall enjoy light reading . . . when, lo! one day I met Susan face to face in the streets of London with a new light in her eye. She had decided on an International Council in Washington, so I had to return with her. . . .

The guests were clapping for her and for Susan. Mrs. Stanton raised her hand for silence, and continued:

Well, I prefer a tyrant of my own sex, . . . for I do believe I have developed into much more of a woman under her jurisdiction . . . than if left to myself reading novels in an easy chair, lost in sweet reveries of the golden age to come without any effort of my own.

SUSAN B. ANTHONY

Spontaneously the guests rose to their feet and clapped and cheered, until at last Susan had to get up and come forward and stand with her hand in Mrs. Stanton's.

"Speech," the women demanded of her.

It was typical of Susan that she spoke just briefly, to thank Mrs. Stanton and the others who had paid compliments to her; it was more typical that she finished by reminding everyone that their real tribute should go to the thousands and thousands of unknown, unsung women of America who were each doing what they could for woman's rights.

As soon as her birthday celebration was over Susan packed her old handbag, bought her railroad tickets and was off for South Dakota for an election campaign. From there she went on and on, from one state to another. As far as she was concerned seventy years of age was a good time to get started.

Five more years of hard work followed. On July 26 she gave a lecture to a huge crowd in an auditorium at Lakeside, Ohio, when suddenly everything went black in front of her eyes. She knew she was fainting. She managed to say one sentence to close her speech, then staggered back to her seat. When she came to after her faint she was thoroughly annoyed with herself.

"If I had pinched myself right hard I would not have fainted," she reproached herself in her diary.

Yet she had to go to bed and it was a month later before she was recovered from what the doctors said was nervous prostration. She got up before she should have, in order to go to New York to prepare for Mrs. Stanton's eightieth birthday celebration.

Christmas was spent with Mary and with Hannah's children and grandchildren, then a campaign for suffrage in

California began, with an urgent request for Susan's help. In the spring of 1896 she was living in the luxurious home of a Mrs. Sargent in San Francisco. Susan rarely had time to enjoy that luxury. She was up in the morning before the servants rose and she came home at night after her hostess was asleep.

Wealthy women could help, but she had found out, long ago, that for the unending day-by-day chores of distributing literature on street corners, stuffing envelopes, organizing meetings and going door to door to speak to housewives, she had to depend upon the small-income housewife and the factory worker.

The California campaign came very close to winning, and Susan returned to Rochester, much heartened.

She had regained her health and optimism and eagerly looked forward to the 1898 National-American Woman's Suffrage convention in Washington. Surely this time they had the push and enough senators on their side to put through the Sixteenth Amendment!

But they had no sooner convened the meeting than news came that the *Maine* had been blown up. The country was now involved in the Spanish-American War, and too busy to think of woman's rights.

It is possible that Susan then guessed she would never see the fulfillment of her dream. No matter! Others would, not only in America, but in all the nations of the world. The only thing to do was keep on working and traveling and speaking. On a trip to England to attend the International Council of Women, she astounded everyone by her vigor. She was equally astonished at the way Emmeline Pankhurst and her daughters were conducting huge shouting demonstrations at the House of Commons in a way unheard-of in America.

SUSAN B. ANTHONY

Good for the Pankhursts, said seventy-nine-year-old Susan B. Anthony, when prim London ladies would have criticized them.

At eighty Susan resigned the presidency of the National-American Association. At the convention women cried and begged her to stay but she spoke firmly to the huge gathering:

> I wish you could realize with what joy and relief I retire from the presidency . . . as long as my name stands at the head I am Yankee enough to feel that I must watch every potato which goes into the dinner pot. . . . I am now going to let go of the machinery but . . . I expect to do more work for woman suffrage in the next decade than ever before.

She added:

> Not one of our national officers ever has made a dollar of salary. I retire on full pay.

Which, of course, was absolutely nothing.

She made it her next task to raise a standing fund of over one hundred thousand dollars for the Association. She knew well how much time was consumed by one individual simply raising enough money to pay for a railroad ticket. Times had changed. Prices had gone up. She was determined that the young people taking over the struggle could use their energy for the cause, not just for begging.

Susan did the begging for them, but it would be a long time before the new president, Carrie Chapman Catt, could have security for the movement. The trouble was, as fast as Susan begged for money, a new need would arise and she would have to spend it.

In 1900, the same year of her official retirement, Susan's brother, Merritt, died suddenly of heart failure. Susan had a slight stroke that same year but was soon up and around and busy, doing her best to conceal her deep grief over her brother. Her doctor recommended that she keep away from crowds, which made her chuckle.

Susan B. Anthony could not walk down the street now without attracting a crowd. The sight of the famous red silk shawl was a magnet.

She took the silk shawl into new places, making speeches to the Knights of Labor, and getting their vote for a resolution for a woman suffrage amendment, and to the International Bricklayers and Masons, who published her speech in their monthly bulletin, reaching sixty thousand people.

By 1902 Susan could feel new life coming into the woman's rights movement—and new hope. She was growing older but she didn't feel old. There was so much work to be done.

Then, on October 26, while she was in Rochester, she answered the doorbell and took the telegram the boy handed her. She opened it and read: "Mother passed away at three o'clock." It was from the daughter of Elizabeth Cady Stanton.

Somehow, while the telegram fluttered to the floor, Susan groped her way upstairs and to her attic workroom. There she sank into a chair and stared around her numbly. All these pictures, all these mementos—and Mrs. Stanton's face or writing in so many of them! Was it possible she could be dead?

Pictures flashed through Susan's mind: their first meeting on the street in Seneca Falls, when pretty little Mrs. Stanton, so young, in her ridiculous bloomer outfit! . . . their first talks, when Mrs. Stanton had been the one to teach and inspire her with an interest in the rights of women—how the two of them had worked on their first petition campaign!

SUSAN B. ANTHONY

Never would she forget Mrs. Stanton standing up in front of the whole state legislature and presenting those petitions and demanding that women have rights over the money they earned and over the children they bore . . .

"Susan? Is thee all right?" It was Mary standing in the doorway, the telegram in her hand, her face anxious and sorrowful. "Won't thee come and eat something?"

Susan shook her head. "I am all right. I'll just sit awhile, if you don't mind."

Mary left her, and Susan sat all that day and most of that night, rocking and thinking and remembering. A lifelong association had snapped. Always, no matter where she had traveled or whatever problems had arisen, she had had Mrs. Stanton to write to or work with; if Susan had suddenly lost the use of her arms and legs she could not have felt more bereft. It seemed to her impossible that Mrs. Stanton could be dead, that she would never see those white curls bobbing against those round cheeks, or hear Mrs. Stanton protesting: "Don't nag me, Susan! I'll get it done somehow." But both of them knew that without the nagging the speech or the history would never get written.

Even now, after all these years, Susan still said "Mrs. Stanton" to herself; never Elizabeth Cady, or just plain Elizabeth.

Their first meeting with that odd, excitable Mr. Train, and those wonderful, wonderful days of putting out the *Revolution*—Susan didn't regret how much they had cost her. Together with Parker Pillsbury they had kept alive the cause at a time when others had demanded it be put aside and forgotten.

At last she roused herself and went to bed and the words of Henry Stanton went with her into sleep: "Here then is work for you, Susan, put on your armor and go forth!" To-

174

morrow there would be work for her and she must again go forth, even though she must go alone now.

Susan came down for breakfast as usual, but Mary noted that her step was not as brisk as usual and, for the first time, that straight back was bowed. Her shoulders stooped.

Nevertheless, she was ready to take up the fight. In the summer of 1904 she attended the International Council of Women in Berlin, where she was feted and cheered and received by the Empress. Susan was not impressed. All that bowing and curtseying . . . ! It would have been more to the point if the Berlin women had handed the Empress a suffrage petition.

The German women acted as if she were just on a sight-seeing tour, and showed her vast public buildings and palaces. Susan eyed them critically. A well-aimed brick thrown through some of those windows might do some good, might wake folks up. When Susan went on to England she again met Emmeline Pankhurst and her daughters; she rejoiced in the fire and spirit they showed. The vote for women obsessed them. Mrs. Pankhurst and her eldest daughter, Christabel, were struck by Susan's great age and by all the years she had worked for suffrage.

"It is unendurable," said Christabel, "to think of another generation of women wasting their lives begging for the vote. We must not lose any more time. We must act!"

Inspired, they did act. They turned their government up by its heels, invading the House of Lords and the House of Commons, marching, smashing windows, going to jail, enduring hunger strikes, going back to jail, keeping things on the boil.

Without knowing it, Susan had helped a great deal to give Emmeline and her daughters the push into forceful, violent action that finally brought them the vote.

SUSAN B. ANTHONY

It was a pity that an ocean separated Susan from the Pankhurst family. They were the kind of women she had long searched for: her kind of people. Instead, she was surrounded by fine, earnest, intellectual, hard-working women, but not the ones to give all and dare all, recklessly and rashly, as she had done and the Pankhursts were doing.

She would have liked to hand over the flame to them, personally. Her own strength was ebbing. When her brother Daniel died in 1904 he left a good-sized legacy to Mary and Susan, which meant Susan had "her own purse" for the first time in her life. But it was too late. She had little use for it, and not much time to spend it.

In 1906 she managed to get up from a sickbed to attend a convention in Baltimore, dress herself in a new crepe de chine dress and go and sit on the platform. Few in the audience knew the effort the eighty-six-year-old woman made to sit upright during the speeches. Julia Ward Howe and Clara Barton, the famous nurse of the Civil War, had the places of honor with her, but the final speech was directed to her:

> To you, Miss Anthony, belongs by right, as to no other woman in the world's history, the love and gratitude of all women in every country of the civilized globe. We, your daughters of the spirit, rise up today and call you blessed. . . .

Susan was glad she had made the effort to come. It was a fitting reward and a final statement of her life.

On March 18, 1906, Susan Brownell Anthony died in the eighty-seventh year of her life at Rochester, with Mary's hand in hers.

Mary, herself, died almost a year later and both sisters left almost everything they possessed to the cause of woman suffrage. However, nothing they left was so imperishable as what happened in the White House in 1920 when President Woodrow Wilson signed the bill which became the Nineteenth Amendment to the Constitution, and which read:

The right of citizens of the United States to vote shall not be denied or abridged by the United States or by any State on account of sex.

Who can deny the possibility that a red-shawled, grey-haired, Quaker ghost did not lean over his shoulder to guide his pen? Who can doubt that same ghost is not hovering over modern women, telling them "the fight's not won yet! Get out there and stir things up!"

BIBLIOGRAPHY

Anthony, Katherine. *Susan B. Anthony: Her Personal History and her Era.* New York: Doubleday & Co., Inc., 1954.

Anthony, Susan B. *An Account of the Procedure of the Trial of Susan B. Anthony.* Rochester, N.Y.: Daily Democrat & Chronicle Press, 1874.

————. Papers and Diaries. Manuscript Division, Library of Congress, Washington, D. C.

Blackwell, Alice Stone. *Lucy Stone: Pioneer of Woman's Rights.* Boston: Little, Brown & Co., 1930.

Bryan, Florence Horn. *Susan B. Anthony: Champion of Woman's Rights.* New York: Julian Messner, 1947.

Dorr, Rheta Childe. *Susan B. Anthony.* New York: Frederick A. Stokes Co., 1928.

Graham, Shirley. *There Was Once a Slave: The Heroic Story of Frederick Douglass.* New York: Julian Messner, 1947.

Harper, Ida Husted. *The Life and Work of Susan B. Anthony.* 3 vols. Indianapolis: The Bobbs-Merrill Co., 1898.

Lader, Lawrence. *The Bold Brahmins: New England's War on Slavery.* New York: E. P. Dutton & Co., 1961.

Lutz, Alma. *Susan B. Anthony.* Boston: Beacon Press, 1959.

Noble, Iris. *Emmeline and Her Daughters: The Pankhurst Suffragettes.* New York: Julian Messner, 1971.

Olmsted, Frederick L. *The Cotton Kingdom.* 2 vols. New York: Mason Bros., 1861.

Parrington, Vernon L. *Main Currents in American Thought.* 3 vols. New York: Harcourt-Brace and Co., 1930.

Phillips, Wendell. *The Constitution, a Pro-slavery Compact.* New York: American Antislavery Society, 1856.

Stanton, Elizabeth Cady. Papers. Manuscript Division, Library of Congress, Washington, D. C.

Stanton, Elizabeth Cady; Anthony, Susan B.; and Gage, Mathilda, eds. *History of Woman Suffrage*. 3 vols. Rochester, N.Y.: Charles Mason, 1881.

INDEX

Anthony, Anna Osborne (sister-
in-law), 106
Anthony, Daniel (father), 7-15,
18, 20-21, 23-27, 32-34, 37, 40-
41, 45, 49, 66, 76, 82, 95, 96,
97, 98, 134
Anthony, Daniel, Jr. (brother),
8, 32, 33, 41, 66, 95, 106, 107,
118, 133, 155
Anthony, Eliza (sister), 8, 14, 18
Anthony, Grandmother, 16
Anthony, Lottie Bolles, 135
Anthony, Lucy (mother), 8-10,
12-13, 18, 21-22, 23-24, 33, 41,
43, 44, 45, 96, 98-99, 106-107,
122, 155, 160
Anthony, Mary (sister), 8, 14,
32, 34, 41, 42, 43, 49, 66, 97,
98-99, 122, 134, 135, 137, 142,
154, 155, 160, 170, 176

Anthony, Merritt (brother), 18,
32, 34, 41, 43, 66, 78-79, 88,
95, 97, 118, 133, 173
Anthony, Susan B.
American Equal Rights Association and, 109-126; antislavery activity of, 77-90; arrested, 137-139; at Canajoharie Academy, 35-39; Civil
War and, 93-108; death of,
176; Draft Riots and, 103-
105; 1853 World's Fair convention and, 60-65; first petition campaign tour of, 65-76;
meets William Lloyd Garrison, 49-50; initial interest in
Woman's Rights, 40-59; last
years of, 160-177; the Philadelphia Centennial and, 155-
159; meets Wendell Phillips,

185

INDEX

ABOUT THE AUTHOR

Writing and traveling fascinate Iris Noble. "In what other profession," she says, "could I carry my office with me? Typewriter in hand, suitcase stuffed with reams of paper, I can be off to work and yet at the same time visit all the exciting places in the world."

She was born in Calgary, Canada, of American parents, and during her early years lived on a ranch in the Crow's Nest Pass. When she was eleven, she moved with her family to Oregon where she attended elementary school in Portland and graduated from Oregon City High School. She majored in English at the University of Oregon and did graduate work at Stanford University in California. She worked as a secretary and as a publicity-advertising director before her marriage to author Hollister Noble in 1941. When they moved soon afterward to New York City, Mrs. Noble began writing magazine articles and gradually moved into books. She has been writing exclusively for young people—biography and fiction—ever since. The urge to travel has sent her throughout Europe, Asia and Africa, researching for new biographical subjects.